"An engagingly readable life guide… A blueprint for helping young people build skills for the modern workplace and for everyday life."

—*Kirkus Reviews*

"Gary Houston's T*he Pie, The Penny & The Pyramid* is a timely, smart and much-needed roadmap for young people to demystify the workplace and take the onramp to success in life. Written in a colorful, no-nonsense style that will resonate with those who employers need to reach most, his book is a must-read for anyone seeking to enter the workforce (and those who want them to succeed)."

—Russ Snyder, Executive Director, California Asphalt Pavement Association, Sacramento CA

"This is a great book for our young employees, whether they are coming from high school or college. Reading this book will help you succeed more and succeed earlier."

—Michael Hutchings, Director of Strategic Development, Clysar, Inc, Clinton, Iowa

"Students leaving university would be well served by reading this book. There is a lot of great information not necessarily covered in the university setting."

—Curtis Berthelot, PhD, President/CEO, PSI Technologies, Saskatoon, SK

"'In a social media-packed world, it's easy to focus on wanting to achieve greatness and be Golden, without seeing all the steps needed to get there. *The Pie, The Penny & The Pyramid* lays out the foundational framework for young graduates and staff entering the workforce. The content brings needed assurance that we do not need to start at the top or always be the best, difficult situations in the workplace happen - that is normal, and the money is sometimes in the journey or experience. I would recommend this book to anyone entering the workforce and currently employed to help clear up common misconceptions about what work should be."

—Kristianne Condell, Operations Manager, GridSME, Sacramento, CA

"*The Pie, The Penny & The Pyramid* is a fun and refreshing guide to living on your own and entering the work force. It brought back memories of my early career, trying to understand where I fit and how business works. I believe people leaving home for the first time, starting their first job or recent graduates will enjoy this fun book guiding them to a meaningful job and a life on their own."

—**Rob Carter, Director of Asphalt & Emulsions, Granite Construction Inc, Reno, NV**

"*The Pie, The Penny & The Pyramid* provides a very accessible framework for negotiating not only the practical realities of the modern workplace, but also for navigating and understanding the emotional component of participation in the workforce. By approaching workforce development with a strategy tailored to the modern young person, Houston offers young people a relatable approach to achieve sustainable success as they transition into adulthood."

—**Ryan Sexton, Senior Director of Programs & Services, Eddy House, Reno, NV**

"There is no doubt that *The Pie, The Penny & The Pyramid* will provide an effective guide for students and others to enter the workforce... I did not want to put the book down. I would recommend this book for high school students because it will guide them on a path to contribute significantly to any organization in which they seek employment."

—**Vivet Beckford-Nelson, Engineering Academy Lead Teacher, Vallejo High School (Vallejo Teacher of the Year 2020, Vallejo, CA)**

The Pie, The Penny & The Pyramid is a MUST READ! Although its target is young adults, high school and university grads, I'd recommend it to their parents and employers, too. To me, Chapter 9 SAAGS (Sadness, Anger, Anxiety, Guilt, Shame/Embarrassment) is a great way to begin the conversation and end the stigma around mental health."

—**Bill G. Williams Author of *Electric Life*, Keynote Speaker, Executive Coach, Toronto, ON**

"Our teens are not the only ones who need direction navigating from school into the workforce. It can be challenging to go beyond surface emotions, help them see their potential, and guide them past their reservations. As a Special Education Paraprofessional who works with young adults, my job is to develop personal relationships as they journey through school. *The Pie, The Penny & The Pyramid* enables me to do that. It helps me see through the eyes of our youth and is a beneficial tool for all the adults in our adolescent's lives."

—Millie Staggs, Special Education SLD/IRR Paraprofessional, Trickum Middle School, Gwinnett County Public Schools, Stone Mountain, GA

"The Pie, The Penny & The Pyramid communicates directly with young people in a relatable and easy to understand way. Any young adult entering the workforce can be coached through Gary Houston's personal humor, historic information and emotional touch to improve the transition from student to career while limiting the fear of the unknown."

—Doug Ford, President, Pavement Coatings Co. Jarupa Valley, CA

"The truly great educators seek to meet their students at their level, and then help them elevate to a higher level. That is exactly what Gary does in his new book… you find a 'Life Coach' in Gary's work that he validates in three ways. He first explains it in a humorous and personal way. Then he re-enforces it with the giants of history, thought leaders like Aristotle become relatable; and then, he makes it actionable for you… Apply it, and you will be better and more successful sooner."

—Brian Majeska, President/CEO, Adventus Materials, Charleston, SC

The Pie, The Penny & The Pyramid

A Guide to Entering the 21st Century Workforce

By Gary Houston

 FriesenPress

One Printers Way
Altona, MB R0G 0B0
Canada

www.friesenpress.com

ISBN
978-1-03-910082-4 (Hardcover)
978-1-03-910081-7 (Paperback)
978-1-03-910083-1 (eBook)

1. BUSINESS & ECONOMICS, CAREERS

Distributed to the trade by The Ingram Book Company

Table of Contents

To Sallie, you are the Art of Integrity, and you have no taste in men.

To Abi & Eli, you should be proud of your growth and path,
and make every day the journey it should be.

To Sam, Isaac, Ethan and Jordyn, you are more M.E. than me,
and more.

To all who have been through our home. You have added so much.

And to George Ferguson (1949 – 2018), my Moral Exemplar.
Extraordinaire.

Introduction

Talent. You have it. We need it. We don't care whether you are tall, small, skinny, or bumpy. We don't care if you are white, black, blue, or purple. We don't care if you have a tail or you have gills. We don't care if you have an accent or a horn. There is room for everyone in our workforce. The workforce is a team across all organizations, cities, countries, and the whole damn planet. We are all pulling together to provide the best life we can for people—without trashing the place. You are an important part of it even if you haven't figured it out yet. We are here to help.

Everyone wants you to succeed. That is probably why you are receiving this book. People care, and they understand that it doesn't matter if you are rockin' the university degree or you are leaving high school and hitting the job market. It doesn't matter if you are from downtown or out of town. You are smart, and you can have a good career and a good life either way. Either way, the sooner you learn how to have a good career, the better off you will be—the better off we will all be. There are a bunch of people who are going to help you out a tremendous amount if you help them out a bit.

This book is simple. You will learn some cool stuff, learn that you already know a bunch of cool stuff, and maybe even smile a bit. You will come out the other end of this thing with skills that will help you for the rest of your long and winding life. We are going to start by giving you some guidelines for how to act and be accepted in the workplace. You will be *Golden*, and people will accept and respect you. They will think you rock.

We are going to build a *Pyramid* that will help you sort things out in the workplace, and in life. We will build a foundation for the pyramid. This is where we will make you *Golden*. We are going to give you the tools to make smart decisions with your money and in your life. We will also look at some of the mistakes everyone makes when they try to figure things out. Doesn't matter if they are smarty-pants university geeks or plain old smart folk. People screw up. Knowing when and how they screw up will help you avoid the same mistakes.

Since we are going to look at other folks, we should learn how to measure what they are made of and what we are made of—it helps. We are going to learn to make *Pies* along the way. We are going to learn that people and situations and wealth and debt are all made up of different ingredients. We are going to bake up some wins by understanding how the different ingredients make up different situations, and how, if you use the right ingredients, you get to have a bigger piece of the *Pie* or get a bigger piece of a bigger *Pie*.

Once we know how to take care of our pies and our pyramid, we will know how to make smart use of our *Pennies*. We are going to look at some mistakes that most of us make when we make decisions. This is going to help us make the most out of what we do have and learn how to get more out of what we will be getting. We are going to meet some really smart people in this book who are going to help us with all of this. It is nice that they have figured a bunch of this stuff out for us.

You are an adult now and you realize that sometimes things suck. It is all *Normal*. We will take a closer look at "normal," and we will take a look at dealing with things that suck, and how to come out the other side with your sanity, and your face all smiley and shiny. We will conquer five negative emotions along the way.

All of this is to get you ready to rock the workplace. We are going to look at organizations in a way that will help you understand how the *Org* really works. We are going to lay out the four parts of your job for you, so you can be the employee with the mostest. The employee that everyone wants. The employee that has a great grip on their *Pyramid* and their *Pennies*.

It doesn't matter whether it is your first job as a young professional or your first part-time job in high school. The rules are essentially the same. Surviving and success are about the same. Success leads to success, and there will be obstacles and failures along the way. There are things you can control and things you can't.

This is not a book about politics, gender, equality, race, or color. If you want to make a poster and protest, please be my guest. The purpose of the book is solely to help all human beings get into the workplace and contribute. You don't have to read this book in order, but it helps. There is a chapter specially for *Fosters*. They will know which one it is.

This is not a book about me; it is about you. But some background about me might help. I have been hiring and mentoring young people for thirty plus years. I have seen them walk in lost and hopeful, helpful and dismal, overconfident and abrupt. I am a university graduate with a couple of degrees. I have written technical papers, taught at universities, and given oodles of presentations across North America. I have been in too many airplanes, eaten a lot of bad-for-me food, and tried to sleep in countless hotels. Lots of *Pie*, enough *Pennies*, and I like my *Pyramid*.

My first job was working in a warehouse in Calgary, Alberta, in the summer of 1980. I was fifteen and clueless. My uncle got me the job. Calgary was desperate for people then, during a business boom. The senior manager seemed to like me, but the superintendent did not. There were three co-workers in the back who I was trying to help. I was not great, but I showed up on time, and was happy to do anything that was asked of me. It was a physical job, so I liked that. But I did not know what to do, so I was waiting for someone to tell me what to do. You will find from this book that all of this is pretty normal. Over time, I have gotten better. I have been a vice president for a couple of different companies, and I can give you some guidance.

I think that first superintendent was like a lot of bosses I have met. They get promoted because they have been there a long time and they work hard. They know how things work and how to get things done, and they are good at what they do. Unfortunately, they don't think they are very smart, so they think everyone should know the job like they do—even if it is their second day. They scoff at everyone and think everyone is a dumbass. You get used to being around these people. Sometimes it takes some skill. A lot of the time, it is frustrating. You will not be alone. We can plan for this.

I went back the following year and worked in the warehouse again. In 1982, I was asked to manage a warehouse. I was seventeen. I went to back to school instead. I worked part time as a busboy, cleaned cars at a car lot, was a security guard and a janitor, worked a summer in the oil fields, and was a pipe extruder for minimum wage after I got my first university degree. I worked throughout school—twenty to sixty hours a week. All before I got my first real job as a chemical engineer. I am now in California. I have a family, and I have been a step, biological, foster, and adoptive parent.

This book is like your career. It is yours, and you can do with it what you like. Scribble in it. Scribble on it. There are lots of blank tables for you to fill out. It will not be hard, and no one is going to grade you on what you put down, or hack on you if you are not neat (but you should be neat). So, scribble in this book like it is your coloring book from when you were five. Your job is going to be a big part of your life and responsible for a lot of your success. The people you are going to meet in the workplace are going to care about you and become like family (most of whom you will like). Take the responsibility to take responsibility now. Doodle some diagrams. Jot your thoughts down. Make some lists. If for some reason it makes you mad, throw it across the room (then go pick it up and pet it). It's your book and it's your life. You can do with it as you like. And as a real start, sign your name on the line below. I have signed mine. Then we can start this little journey. After you think you are done, tuck it in a drawer or a shoebox and you can show it to your kid in twenty years.

One of our key dudes, Aristotle, said, "Well begun is half done."

Let's begun.

Gary Houston

Gary Houston   _____

                                              You

Glossary

Ari – Aristotle (384 – 322 BC) was a very famous Greek philosopher from 2,500 years ago. He thought a lot about living a good life. We are going to use his thoughts as a foundation for a successful career.

Aristotle and the Doctrine of the Golden Mean – Aristotle thought one should strive to live between excess and absence. Somewhere in the middle (the ***Mean***). As you learn to operate in the mean, you can take your behavior to be truly virtuous (***Golden***) by copying others (***Moral Exemplars***) who have already figured it out. A sort of fake-it-to-make-it approach.

Golden – When you learn to operate in the ***Mean***, and then to optimize your behavior to be virtuous and to stand out and be respected, you are ***Golden***. You definitely want to be ***Golden*** in the workplace, and in life.

Goldilocks – ***Goldi*** is every person that works with you in the workplace. They all need their stuff just right. ***Goldi*** might be a 300 lb. scary dude. Wherever possible, you need to give ***Goldi*** what they need, when they need it, how they need it, and as legibly as you can. ***Goldi*** can be a great champion for you in the ***Org***. Make ***Goldi's*** day. He or she needs your help. You can help them have a great day.

Kahn – Dr. Daniel Kahneman (1934 – present) is an Israeli-born American psychologist who has won the Nobel Prize in Economics. Dr. Kahneman is best known for his work in decision-making, judgments, and behavioral economics. We will use ***The Kahn*** to learn about how people think in the workplace and in life. We can use ***The Kahn's*** rules of thumb to avoid some of the mistakes all humans have a tendency to make.

M.E. – You are your own moral exemplar when you are your own ***M.E.*** When you can be the one who other people want to copy, they want to act like you. You become the one who knows how to act in public, who knows how to talk to people you do not know, and who can handle new situations.

Maz – Abraham Maslow (1908–1970) was an American psychologist who is best known for developing the *Hierarchy of Needs* as a motivational tool. It is presented in pyramid form and represents people progressing from needing basic human necessities, through more advanced social and emotional recognition. We will use *"the Maz"* as shorthand to represent our pyramid as it relates to our career, our life, and our money.

Mean – Being mean is being average in your behavior. You do not have to be the greatest, fastest, or loudest, or the one with the most expensive wardrobe. Being *Mean* is a great place to start, and according to Ari's *Doctrine of the Golden Mean,* you can start by being *Mean* in your behavior and learn to tailor your behavior to each situation and to your skills.

Moral Exemplar – Ari recommends that you find a *Moral Exemplar* to copy. These are the people who just seem to know how to do things right. They know to act in public or in the workplace. How to handle other people. How to talk to people they don't know.

Normal – Many random events (like height, weight, foot size, roll of dice) follow a pattern referred to as a *normal distribution.* This is a bell-shaped distribution where more events are average than not average, and the further from average the events are, the less likely they are to occur. We will use *Normal* to refer to situations in life that are mostly average and not likely to stray too far from average—most of the time. Those events that are far from average—either super good or super bad—range from rare to very rare.

Org – This is the living, breathing organization you will be working for. It has several recognizable features, and Goldilock's needs are flowing through every pore of the company.

Pie – The *Pie* is another distribution we refer to. The *Pie* is used as a tool to divide up people, time, and money into various characteristics with different proportions. The value of the *Pie* is in learning to see the diversity of people and situations and learning to work within their wide range of slices.

PEELS – On the first day of work, you should remember your *PEELS*:

- Pen – bring a pen and all your information,

- Engage – become involved with the staff and other workers,

- Empathy – try to understand what others are feeling as they are meeting you, and remember that they are just as nervous about meeting you,

- Listen – listen to the speaker(s), and

- Smile – try to smile.

Pennies – The **Pennies** we refer to are those we earn from employment. They are fewer than we think they should be, and far more valuable than we know. We need to learn to treat them as the scarce resources they are as we address our **Pyramid** and our **Pie**.

Pyramid – The **Pyramid** we refer to is constructed from Maslow's *Hierarchy of Needs*. We are modifying it to fit our work life and where we are in our careers. The **Pyramid** also is used as a guide to how we should distribute the money we earn.

SAAGS – The **SAAGS** are five negative emotions in the workplace. Strategies to recognize and deal with Sadness, Anxiety, Anger, Guilt, and Shame/embarrassment are presented.

Social Meds – All the social media channels are referred to as **Social Meds**. People use them like they are medicine, but they do not generally cure anything.

WYSIATI – This acronym is from *The Kahn*, and it refers to, "What you see is all there is." **WYSIATI** reminds us there is no magic in the workplace, and people can only know the information they have been given.

CHAPTER 1

In the Beginning . . .

Welcome. We are going to prepare you to be successful in your job, in your career, and in your life. You already have the tools and doohickeys you need. You are already smart. We are going to help you sharpen those tools and doohickeys, organize those tools and doohickeys, and use them like you are a virtuoso doohickey player. You are going to be **Golden**.

We are going to help you understand how to get the most out of your **Pie**, so that you have as many **Pennies** as possible when you get to the top of your **Pyramid**. We are going to help you build a rock-solid foundation for that **Pyramid** based on you being **Golden**, and it is a foundation of stuff you mostly already know. We build your **Pyramid** on a pretty much **Golden** foundation. **Golden** will end up feeling pretty average for you. What you do with **Golden** will be, well, **Golden**.

Your career will play the biggest supporting role in your life. It will support you. It will support your family. It will help your friends. It will help you help your city/town and country. It doesn't matter what has happened so far in your life. You can be successful. Getting off to a great start is surprisingly easy. We just need to understand a few things that you already know.

Let's model[1] you and your job:

---

1   In this case, a model is not the buff, hot kind with really good hair products. Sorry, you will just have to get used to that kind of disappointment in this book. The model is a simple description we use to communicate an idea.

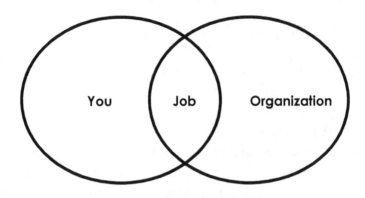

Figure 1.1 – The Intersection of Your Life

The diagram above shows us that the job is an intersection between you and a company, or organization. (We will refer to the organization as *Org* 'cuz I don't like typing big words.) It is natural to think, "How do I get to that intersection? How do I get a job?" We will talk about that, and you can head straight there if you want.[2] Before we get to all this *Pie*, *Penny*, and *Pyramid* stuff, and applying for and getting a job, we should first meet the main cast of characters who will help organize all this for us.

To increase your chances of success, both in attaining success and realizing what success looks like, we are going to take a look at each of the people mentioned in Table 1.1 and how they fit into different parts of our model: You, the job, and the organization.

---

2   See Chapter 14, Getting That Job. While that part is exciting, Chapter 10 is one of the more boring ones. Just sayin'. I would read the rest first. But it is your book, and it is your choice.

Table 1.1 – Cast of Characters

Aristotle - **Ari** (Chapter 4)	Ancient Greek: 384 – 322 BC	One of our first philosophers who will help with what goes into a good **Pie**	Identified the good life, became **Golden** by starting out average
Abraham Maslow - **The Maz** (Chapter 5)	American psychologist: 1908 – 1970	Architect of the Hierarchy of Needs, which we will use for our **Pyramid**	Identified what is important and how to recognize what is important
Dr. Daniel Kahneman – **The Kahn** (Chapter 8)	American decision-maker: 1934 – present	Nobel Prize-winning thinker who will help us with our **Pennies** and more	Identified mistakes people make when they think
You	2000-ish to beyond	Our next success	Living the **Golden Mean**, working on being an **M.E.**[3]

---

3   M.E. is not me; it's you. You want to be an M.E. I will be me. You be an M.E., which is not me. You can do much better than me.

3

Success

We are not worried right now about having a bunch of money or being a celebrity. We want to have enough money, we want some security, and we want to be respected. If we get rich and we become the next Internet *sensei*, great. Good for you. Coolio. Our goal right now is to get ourselves on the right track, pay our bills, and save a bit for emergencies, for the future, and for some of the **Normal** things and some of the good things that happen in life. This will make an attractive package to maybe finding a compatible mate so that you can be **Golden** together. And maybe stay together.

In order to achieve all that, we are going to avoid some things. We are going to make choices that help us avoid harm, we are going to have the willpower to make sure we are not going to be hungry, and we are going to make decisions that ensure we will not be homeless. And there is our goal. It is simple, and you already knew it. Maybe you never quite looked at it that way before.

Avoid harm, hunger, and homelessness.

If we avoid those three pitfalls, and we make decisions that are always moving us away from them, then we are always moving towards a better place, a good life.

The great thing about living in the country we live in is that living even an average life is a great life, compared to history, and compared to many other parts of the world today. If you make avoiding harm, hunger, and homelessness part of your decisions, you are going to be on a path to a successful life. Whether you are downtown or out of town, whether you are out of high school or totally schooled, it is simple, it is fundamental, and you are smart enough to know it. Good. So that was easy.

You, the Job, and the Organization

Let's look at you, the job, and the organization.

You

We hope to make you into an **M.E.** We want *you* to get to know *you* from a work perspective, and what you need to look like in order to contribute to the organization where you will work. We are going to use some building blocks, some platforms, and some ideas to help you become who you want to become—successful, respected, and financially secure. We are going to build your life pyramid with the **Maz**, talk to **Ari** on how to be **Golden** and **Mean**, and see if we can learn from the **Kahn** how to make better decisions. So, we can be a **Moral Exemplar**[4] at home, at work, and in society. You don't have to go to Harvard or some other schmancy gazillion-dollar school. You can live a great life just by doing well at work. It can be **Normal**.

Figure 1.2 – M.A.K. > M.E.

We want you to understand where you are, how to act, and how to think, and then see how that becomes contribution. More contribution leads to more success, more security, more safety, and less chance of harm, hunger, and homelessness.

---

4   Moral Exemplar sounds cool. It should be on a T-shirt with a staff, or a wand. Like a Nimbus ME from when you were a kid.

The Job

There are steps to take for success in your first job. The first step is understanding that the job is an intersection between you and your employer. (I hope you didn't miss the big diagram on page 1, Figure 1.1; if you need to, go back and look at it—we'll wait.) You are part of the organization, and the organization is part of you. You have to engage with the organization, and you have to participate with all the parts of the organization. The organization will give you money to do that. It is one of the conditions of employment. We can break down most jobs into four components:

1. *Duties* – These are the things you are hired to do, on your own, by yourself, with little to no direction. Another word might be *work*. Jobs have different levels of work, but they all have some. You might want to call these duties, chores, or assignments. You get it. Don't screw up.

2. *Administration* – This part of your job is more important than you think. These are information things you *must* do to keep the organization rolling along without you causing problems. Things like filling out your timecards accurately and on time, filling out your payroll, tax, and benefits paperwork—all of your personal information—on time, and do it legibly. Also, ask for time off well before the requested time off (which you should rarely request, because people need you there helping).

3. *Data* – Organizations run on data. Whether it's a huge company like McDonald's or Walmart, or Miss Daisy's Dog Grooming around the corner, data has to be captured, saved, and presented to help the decision-makers in the organization. This may include completing forms to show how much raw materials you used or how many sales calls you made, or completing paperwork to show you are getting the right training and that you have the right safety equipment. Maybe it is paperwork that shows you did all the right things with the waste created in manufacturing to show the government that the organization is not polluting the world, and to show the organization that you are not creating

problems, and that you can account for everything you do, every-thing you use, everything you sell. All the pennies you touch, all the supplies, all the finished goods, all the inventory. Data covers your butt and everyone else's.

4. *Communication* – If you do a great job and nobody knows about it, did you do a great job? If you need help and you don't ask anyone for help, are you just a lazy schmuck? If you don't under-stand what someone is saying, are you going to end up doing the right thing? You need a simple strategy to communicate if you are going to participate.

We will also talk about the steps for getting a job. We are talking basic, first-job stuff. Get your big-person undies on and go make some money. Get some respect for yourself. The ultimate job, dream of a lifetime, comes later. Right now, we are trying out our adult undies and learning not to leave marks.

The Organization

Do you know how an organization works? We are going to look at it in a new way. One that will help you succeed and give you an idea of how to take the four parts of the job and satisfy everyone in the workplace. There are even these little greebles named *Goldilocks*, and we will help you satisfy them too. Organizations or companies are referred to in many different ways. They can mean so many things to so many people, it is no wonder they take on a life of their own. Well, they are alive and should be treated as such. Just like we identify our family members by different titles, they are all family. We have different terms for different organizations (businesses, corporations, firms, establishments, partner-ships, non-profits, etc.)—they are all *Org*. We should note that the term *business* evolved from the term "busy-ness." The state of doing something. Note that it started out as the state of being busy. Not the state of you standing around surfing on your phone, scratching your butt crack.

It doesn't matter what we call it, and it doesn't matter whether it is a huge national company like Home Depot or Microsoft, or a small cupcake company, or a non-profit puppy shelter, or a government department.

They all have the same parts, and they all need people to come and help, to contribute, and to add value.

The organization should start to feel like a real living thing. And it is. So, we will call it **Org** and draw it in all its coolness.[5]

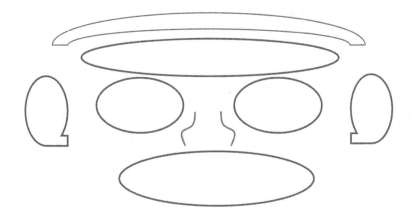

Figure 1.3 – Org

Org is kind of like a family tree, but we are going to look at the **Org** tree and see how it all works together to form a living, breathing, feeling thing. A thing you are going to be a **Golden** part of, and you are going to be **Golden** at.

To get to the point where we get the point, we are going to take a bit of a look at you, and you with your family and friends. We are going to build a foundation for you to build a **Pyramid** on. Then we are going to build your **Pyramid**. If we make our decisions consistent with our **Pyramid**, we stay away from harm, hunger, and homelessness.

Pennies

And how much money is enough? It isn't that hard to figure out. We can divvy up your **Pie** and figure out what it means to make fifteen dollars per hour, three thousand dollars a month, or seventy-five thousand dollars

---

5   I am a horrible artist. My sister is an awesome artist. This is the best I could do. But we will fill in the parts of **Org** later in Chapter 10, and it will make more sense. I hope.

per year. The **Pennies** will come, and when they get here, we want to know what to do with them. Some simple rules of thumb (thank you, Dr. Kahneman) and you will have a platform, or a simple spreadsheet, that is useful, real, and long-lasting. Budgets are great and you should sort of have one. Those kids who sat in the front row and always had their hand up in class? Maybe they have an actual detailed budget—what else did they have to do? Yes, we should all have a budget. What does a budget really have to do? It has to help us meet our goals. Remember the part about avoiding harm, hunger, and homelessness? Once we have learned about our **Pie** and our **Pyramid**, then making money decisions are surprisingly easy.

The questions are: How do you make big decisions like, when is it time to move out? How do you decide whether to save a bit of money or buy another set of ear pods? How do you decide whether to take out a loan? When we get to the Math of Kahn in Chapter 8, we will understand how to make good decisions, whether they are big or small.

There is nothing hard or complex about what we are about to do. It just takes a little grown-up effort, a little organization, and a willingness to do what is right. If we do this right, we can tie it all together and not trip over our own feet as we go along. You have a **Normal** chance of living a life that you can be proud of, and becoming a person who feels good about what you do. Your Mom might even like you.

CHAPTER 2
Goals

This book will help you survive, prosper, and succeed. You will feel good about it. To do that, you have to recognize it. You have to be willing to chase it.

Figure 2.1 – What We Seek

While we are seeking what we are pursuing, we need to confirm what we need to avoid. If we do it well enough, we can use it as a platform to shape most of the decisions we are going to make as an adult. What do we want to avoid?

Figure 2.2 – What We Avoid

In Table 2.1, put in your own words. What are you going to avoid that will help you get to your goals? What are you going to seek so that you can feel good about yourself, and you can feel you are succeeding? Go ahead, give it a shot. This is just a warm-up.

Table 2.1 – Avoiding and Seeking

Avoid	Avoid	Seek	Seek
Harm			Survival
Hunger			Prosperity
Homelessness			Success

There is no magical way to live a perfect life. A perfect life doesn't likely exist. But we can make a lot of small decisions that support your table above. Within this book, we are going to make decisions to avoid harm, hunger, and homelessness. If we do that, we will be closer to the prosperity and success we are shooting for.

Whether you think in terms of your pieces of the *Pie*, having lots of *Pennies*, or where you will be on your *Pyramid*, not everything will go perfectly. That is *Normal*. We want to prepare you for that.

It is also assured that your thoughts will change on your pieces of the *Pie*, how many *Pennies* you need, and where you are on your *Pyramid*. How we measure things is really important. We want to make sure we get our starting point right. Are we worrying about the right things? Do we have the right goals? Do we measure everything in real terms (how much money do we have)? Or do we measure things in relative terms? (do I have more money than my friends/parents/siblings/Kanye)?

Let's look at your goals for today (or tomorrow, if it is too late). What about your goals for this week?

Table 2.2 – Goals for Today and This Week

	Goals for Today	Goals for This Week
1.		
2.		
3.		
4.		

Here are two questions about what you entered above:

1. Can we measure how successful you are in attaining those goals?

2. Were your goals in support of avoiding harm, hunger, and homelessness?

Avoiding harm, hunger, and homelessness may be really trivial when you think of where you are right now. Maybe you are in your bedroom that your parents have provided you for the past eighteen to thirty-five years. Cool. Great. It won't always be like that.

A lot of things in life are relative—that is, we compare them to other things. We continually compare one thing to another, make a decision, and then go with the thing we decided on. What if our comparison is wrong? What if our decision is wrong? What if things are not as they seem? How do you compare your goals to other goals? Look at the lines below. Which one is longer?

Figure 2.3 – Müller-Lyer Illusion

It turns out the two lines are the same length. It is an illusion. It is commonly referred to as the Müller-Lyer Illusion. The arrowheads (which are generally referred to as chevrons, and chevron is French for rafters) change how we perceive the length of the lines. And Müller-Lyer[6] was one dude, not two. Did you assume two? Interesting. We made a quick reasonable assumption, but we were wrong.[7] When we compare things to each other, we can get it wrong. We might measure something wrong, or we might measure the wrong thing.

Your success in the workplace depends on how hard you work, how much people like and respect you, and how much luck you get—and whether the luck is good or bad. You are probably not going to get all the *Pennies*, or the entire *Pie*. Does that mean you fail? How much do you need to be a success? How much of what? What do you really need? You do not need to know the answer right now. You just need to start something.

What do you need right now from your job?

_____

_____

_____

What do you need in two years from your job?

_____

_____

_____

A good question to ask yourself is, what do you need right now from your job? Do you just want some money so you can go do stuff with your tribe or your BFF or your honey-boo-boo? Or are you building a resume or wanting to train in your chosen field? All good answers. Jot down your thoughts in the table above, and jot down what you will need in two years. Your needs will change. It is best to get going today, so you are ready when your needs do change.

Here is a dirty little secret that goes a long way toward achieving success and avoiding harm, hunger, and homelessness. Work is fun. Maybe not in a Six Flags or Disneyland sort of way. More like an "I am an adult, and I accomplished some things, and I helped a bunch of people at

---

6   Franz Carl Müller-Lyer was originally Franz Xavier Hermann Müller, and he was born in 1857 in Baden Baden, Germany. He presented the illusion in 1889. He was Baden-ass, or Baden-ess, or Baden-Baden-ass.

7   We *Kahn*'d ourselves. We will learn about that later.

work who were looking for help, and these people seem to appreciate me" sort of way.

Enjoying work is a great sign that you are maturing as an adult. It is eating healthy versus eating candy. You can sit on your phone and watch cat videos, which does nothing for you or anyone else, or you can go to work, make some money, and help people. You choose.

Some days, work sucks. Some days, life sucks. But most days are pretty good, and the only way you get to find out what tomorrow is like is to get through today. Suck it up. Life is *Normal*.

Success

What do you need to consider yourself a success? What does success look like? Look at the table and fill in some words on being successful.

What will be signs that you are successful in your job or career?

_____

_____

_____

_____

Did you identify signs of success or signs of celebrity? There is a big difference. Celebrity just means you are well known—what does that do for 'ya? How many celebrities can you think of who became train wrecks? Would you really want to live like that? Is there anything better than celebrity that could satisfy you and make you feel good about yourself, and make your family proud of you?

How much money do you think you need to make in your first job? How many hours will you work? Where will you work, and what will you do?

Also, how important is education to your success? You can be successful regardless of the level of education you have. Believe me or don't. The workforce rewards people who are great workers (the *Golden*, the *M.E.s* we are going to learn about). The rewards are smaller than you think they should be, they take longer than they should, and they are waaaayyy more valuable than you realize. Not bigger. More valuable.

15

Having more education may help you rise higher in companies, into the management structure, if that is what you want to do. Having more education usually means you do less physical work than you would otherwise do, which may or may not be attractive to you. If you are a schmuck, dufus, jerk, lazy ass, jackwagon, dolt, obnoxious whiner, bitchface, or whatever, it doesn't matter how much education in the world you have. No one is going to want to work with you.

The opposite side of that is if you are a great person and a great worker. If you are **Golden**, as we will define, and an **M.E.**, it doesn't matter how much education you have. People are going to want to work with you. You will likely end up having people work *for* you (even though you might continue to consider yourself as working with them). You will get the raises (smaller than you think they should be, more valuable than you know). You will get the promotions. You will get the respect. Does that kind of success have value for you?

Table 2.3 – First Job

First Company:	Pay:
Job:	Hours per week:
Is this success or failure?	

Regardless of what the job is, how much you are making, and how much you are working, you are moving away from harm, hunger, and homelessness. That is what matters, and that puts you on the path to success. That makes you an adult.

Caution

Is having a family (kids, puppies, goldfish) part of success? Very cool if it is; no problem if it isn't. It is your life. You need to know what the Wealth Killers[8] are and you need to avoid them. The **Golden** life will need you to use your brain and not bring kids into the world unless you and your partner are healthy. You need to graduate high school and get a job. Then you can think about getting a life partner or making your partner your life partner. You need to have that life partner before you can think about bringing children into the mix. At a minimum:

1. Graduate high school

2. Get a job

3. Get a life partner

4. Have child (or not)

To be clear, no #4 before #3, no #4 before #2, no #4 before #1. No excuses. Better yet, get some more schooling before #4. There is no rush to bring babies into this world. You are going to live a long life. If you don't have a life, get your own life before you bring another life into it. We will talk about the platforms in your life a little later, and you can figure out where to fit the little bambinos in.

More About Success

If you decide the only way you will be a success is to be worth a bazillion dollars and you only get half a bazillion, did you fail? Was that your only measuring stick? Did you turn into the old glass-half-empty pouty pants? Or do you think you need to be a social media star with followers who want to know when you pee?

Every real champion has successes and failures. Athletes spend their lives trying to get one Olympic medal or one Super Bowl ring. Entertainers get one Oscar or Grammy or nothing. Are they a failure if they don't get

---

8   See Chapter 12, Wealth Killers. You have to read it.

stardom? Maybe it depends on whether their arrows are pointing outside or inside. Or it depends on how you measure and what you measure.

I have spent a good bit of time coaching kids in team sports. It hurts like hell to lose the gold medal game, but in time, you realize you were in the championship. Competition is part of us. It is okay to compete. I have told many players and parents that silver medals get better with age. All the little wins along the way pay you back for the days of *ginormous* failure. Learning how to be *Golden* when you win is a skill you need to develop if you do not already have it in your pocket. If you missed the game-winning free throw or struck out while pinch-hitting with two outs in the ninth inning, remember, you were the one picked for the task. That says a lot about how much you are valued. Did you try out for cheerleading and not make it? That takes a lot of guts. Guts grow into maturity. If you forgot your line on stage, remember how hard you practiced. Practice is how you get poise. Maybe you got a bad outcome after some really hard, great work. Did you help someone today? Open a door, smile at an elderly person? That is success, and it matters more than you think.

We are going to define losing and failure as two different events entirely. They both feel like crap. If you lose, someone or something was better than you. Maybe their luck was good luck, and you had bad luck. It was a moment in time that you prepared for, and it didn't quite work out as you would have liked. If you fail, you didn't show up. You didn't try. You sat on your ass knowing you should do something, but you couldn't push off the couch, straighten your legs, and walk towards being *Golden*. If you are mature, you can lose, feel like crap, and live to succeed another day. If you fail, you are still on the couch, you are not closer to maturity, and you are much closer to harm, hunger, and homelessness.[9]

I asked a question of a minor league coach (one step below the professional league): If your players don't make it to the pros, do they view themselves as failures? Sadly, quite a few do. But consider the journey. I bet those players have traveled all over North America or the world.

---

9   We are going to talk about how to get $%#& done when we learn how to deal with procrastination. We can put it off until then, or you can go have a look right now. I hope you found that funny.

And someone has paid for most or all of it. They have stayed in hotels; traveled on buses, trains, and airplanes; eaten all kinds of food; and met all kinds of people. They have worked extremely hard at something they love doing. And they've been looked up to, admired, and respected. They picked up extremely valuable skills along the way—hard work, dedication, reliability.

Most people do not realize it, but the value is in the journey. To get really, really good, they must have worked hard. They need discipline. They need to be smart and they need to get along with teammates, coaches, referees, officials, fans, and opponents. All extremely valuable characteristics. So even if you don't win the Oscar, the Grammy, the ESPY, the Super Bowl, or the Pulitzer, or have a number-one hit, or have four thousand pairs of shoes in your crib, you can add a lot of value to yourself, your family, and others just by working hard and caring about and helping those around you while on your journey. If we do it right, there is a good chance we will have money and we will have security, and we will see where that puts us on the hillside of our **Pyramid**.

The value is in the journey.

Being **Golden** isn't about winning championships or earning major awards or being a GOAT. Being **Golden** is about being solid and reliable, learning every day, and contributing. The **Kahn** will tell us that acquiring excellence is all practice and feedback. Good luck helps. Whatever you are practicing will transfer into the workplace. You are always a good investment.

Workplace Journey

In the workplace—and you will hear this more than once from me—we need your help. You have something to offer. Even if you and I do not know what it is yet. What you have to offer is going to change many times over your work life. What we need to figure out is what you need to offer **Org** so you start off on the right foot. And it will really help if we can figure out what to do with the little, tiny, tiny, tiny slice of **Pie** you get to take home. Although there is nothing bigger and sweeter than your first paycheck, there are also fewer things more disappointing than how much the government takes from you, even on your first paycheck.

But let's back up. Why are we going to get a job? Well, money—we will talk about that. To survive—we will talk about that too. Some of us just like to work. Give me something broken, I will fix it. Give me something to build, I will build it. Give me something to cook, I will cook it. And most of us have a need to contribute. To add to things. To help. To grow, to learn, to teach. You might not think you have much right now, but I have seen it time and time again—you do. You probably want to contribute; you don't realize you already are.

We now know that measuring what we are doing and how well we are doing is relative and inexact. That may be a bit of a bummer, but it gives us a bit of a break. We do not worry about measuring every detail to the bazillionth of an inch. We do not need to measure against an Ivy League stock bitchzillionaire, or the latest Wapper with a hundred million followers, or a twelve-year-old tech geek. We just need to make some general statements that give us a direction to start.

Consider the following:

Be an adult

1. Finish high school

2. Get a job

3. Get a partner

4. Make babies (or not)

Bonus Points

5. Get more schooling

6. Keep your partner

7. Make healthy babies (or do not make babies)

Be *Golden*

8. Contribute. Enjoy helping.

We now have a plan.

CHAPTER 3
You

Are you ready right now to get a job? Well, whether you are or not, let's start by having a look at you. You are your biggest and best asset;[10] at some level it's all you've got, and the great thing is, it's all you've got. You are what you have to offer to a company in order to get a decent, reasonably paying job that will earn you money and respect. It will help you help your family. Even if that family doesn't exist yet. It will help you make more money. You generally start at the bottom when you are starting your career. Consider it training, like going to the gym or beginner's yoga. You have to start with the easy stuff to progress to the higher-paying, harder stuff. You have to start at the bottom to learn how to make more money. We will look at how you get a job with what you've got, and we will take stock of what you have to offer.

You are somewhere in the process of becoming an adult. Maybe just started, maybe almost there. Maybe you are thirty-five and wearing pajamas all day, living at your Mom's place, and playing video games in the basement, and you need a kick in the ass to grow up. Maybe you are sixteen and ready for the next challenge in life. Maybe you are just graduating Harvard, ready to kick ass and take names. Maybe you need some money to help your family make ends meet. Whatever your situation, the steps you need to take are the same.

Work Ready

Are you interested in going to work and starting to make money? Fill out the table on the next page. Just read through the options and circle

---

10   An asset is something that has value—like money or gold. Or you. You have value. Lots of it.

the most appropriate response today (remember, it's your book, your life). It may give you something to think about. We will deal more with your responses later on. Right now, we just want to make sure you are ready to enter the workforce. We want to start by determining whether you are ready, willing, and able to get a job. Getting a job looks great when it is out there in the distance, far away like a mirage or a dream. As you get closer, it gets a little more real and a little tougher to commit to all the details you have to take care of to search for, apply for, and get hired for a real paying job—whether part-time or full-time; after high school or after college.

As an adult, you can look at Table 3.1, the Pre-Employment Checklist, and ask yourself whether you are just thinking about getting a job, whether you have decided to get a job, and whether you are committed to going through the process you need to go through to start bringing home a paycheck. You need to answer whether you are adult enough to get a paying job. Start with the "Things to Do" section and circle the appropriate answer for each question. Sign your name (legibly). It is an adult commitment to yourself that you are going to do what you need to do to enter the workforce. It is a big step. It may not seem like much, but it is more important than you think. The workplace will require you to do what you say you are going to do. Here is the first step.

There is some personal information you need to gather so that you have it ready when you start filling out application forms. There is more on that later. Also, you need to be honest with yourself about whether you can pass drug-screening tests, which are used by over half of the employers in the United States before they will hire you. If you have a criminal record or a DUI (driving under the influence), you may have to go beyond this book and seek extra help to find permanent employment. Criminal records, drugs, and DUIs have far-reaching consequences. You will understand more about risky behavior in the workplace and in life as you go through this book. If you are clean in all three areas, you are already ahead of many people who have short-circuited their careers through their reckless decisions and actions.

Table 3.1 – Pre-Employment Checklist

Things to Do			
Thinking About applying for work	Yes	Maybe	No
Decide to Apply for work	Yes	Maybe	No
Commit to Apply for work	Yes	Maybe	No
Signature: _____ Date:			
Adult enough to get a job	Yes	Maybe	No

Gather Necessary Information & Documents

Birth Certificate	Yes	No	
Passport	Yes	No	N/A
Social Security Card	Yes	No	
Work Visa/Green Card (if needed)	Yes	No	N/A
Driver License	Yes	No	
Drivers Record	Yes	No	
Resume	Yes	No	

Ability to Pass Background Checks:

Drug (Urine Analysis)	Yes	No
Drug (Saliva)	Yes	No
Drug (Hair)	Yes	No
Crime (misdemeanor)	Yes	No
Crime (felony)	Yes	No
DUI	Yes	No

How did you do? Are you ready and willing? Are you able? We will come back to the necessary documents later in Chapter 14, You and Your Job, when we talk about the process of getting a job. We will talk about the importance of things like background checks and drug testing in Chapter 12, Wealth Killers. Hopefully, these are non-issues for you. You need your eyes wide open.

Job Choices

Let's look at the types of jobs you think you can do right now. What are you willing to do? This will help you in a job search. Just circle whether you find each type of job in Table 3.2 desirable, or totally not. Somewhere between 1 and 5. You can add other jobs you might really, really want, or jobs you totally do not want to touch at the bottom of the table.

Table 3.2 – List of Starting Jobs

Type of Job					
	Desirable		OK		No
Retail	1	2	3	4	5
Fastfood	1	2	3	4	5
Service	1	2	3	4	5
Clerical	1	2	3	4	5
Labor	1	2	3	4	5
Technical	1	2	3	4	5
Professional	1	2	3	4	5
Manufacturing	1	2	3	4	5
Trades	1	2	3	4	5
Repairing	1	2	3	4	5
Fixing	1	2	3	4	5
Maintaining	1	2	3	4	5
Landscaping	1	2	3	4	5
Agriculture	1	2	3	4	5
Cleaning	1	2	3	4	5

Cooking	1	2	3	4	5
Serving	1	2	3	4	5
Selling	1	2	3	4	5
Computer - Using	1	2	3	4	5
Computer - Operator	1	2	3	4	5
Computer - Support	1	2	3	4	5
Computer - Installation	1	2	3	4	5
Security	1	2	3	4	5
Other:_____	1	2	3	4	5
Other:_____	1	2	3	4	5
Other:_____	1	2	3	4	5
Other:_____	1	2	3	4	5
Other:_____	1	2	3	4	5

Are you willing to do the jobs that are available to you, or are you going to wait until the job that you want comes to you? Are you willing to do a job that you think is beneath you? Have you been told how special, how wonderful, and how smart you are for as long as you can remember? Do you expect things to be handed to you? Does that mean you will head straight to the boss's chair? Ready to run a Fortune 100 tech company? Give Musk or Zuckerberg your wisdom? I hope you understand there are still things to learn, still skills to acquire, still growing to do.

Pennies

The money you make during your career will be based on the actual job you do. How much money you make will be based on many things, much more than just how much university education you have. There are a tremendous number of jobs available to you that are great jobs, providing great opportunities, great careers, and great pay.

There are a lot of factors that go into how much money a job pays. There are lots of jobs that require a university degree, but don't pay a lot of money. They can still be great jobs, but maybe there are reasons why they do not pay a zillion dollars. Note that there is a great difference in what a job pays that depends on where you live (location, location, location). Parts of the country, like New York City or Los Angeles, pay much higher than a small city in the central US (cost, cost, cost). There is value in checking out the relative **Pennies** that jobs pay, compared to each other.

Let's take a moment to consider who makes how much money. Look at Table 3.3. Who *should* make more money? Why should they make more money? You can grab some descriptive word from Table 3.4 if you want.

Table 3.3 – Compensation Comparison

	Choose which one should make more money	Why? Write down a couple of descriptive words
Lawyer vs. farmer		
Nurse vs. teacher		
Miner vs. store clerk		
Data entry clerk vs. McDonald's worker		
Restaurant hostess vs. restaurant server		
Office manager vs. electrician		
Laborer vs. surgeon		
Pilot vs. bus driver		
Corrections officer vs. accountant		
Equipment operator vs. landscaper		
Stockbroker vs. police officer		
Hair stylist vs. childcare worker		
Salesperson vs. engineer		
Oilfield worker vs. cook		
Laborer vs. plumber		
Ten-year mechanic vs. three-year mechanic		
Doctor vs. store clerk		

If you completed Table 3.3, you probably identified a few words that described a quality in one job that is valued more than a quality in another job. In work terms, these are called *compensable factors*—these are things that people get compensated (paid) for. Some compensable factors are listed in Table 3.4. I have left some rows at the bottom for you to add your own compensable factors. In the second column, place each factor in relative order of importance. In the third column, identify the factor that you have the most of, down to the one you have the least.

Table 3.4 – Compensable Factors

Compensable Factor	Importance (number from 1 to 7, with 1 being the most important)	List the qualities you have (from 1 to 7, with 1 being the quality you have the most of)
Expertise		
Education		
Experience		
Fancy-schmancy (working with large $ amounts or super-secret things)		
Gross/danger (working in or with unpleasant things)		
Specialized/remote (removed from civilization)		
Effort		

From Table 3.4, hopefully you see that you are not likely to make huge dollars to start. As we have said, we all start out at the bottom. The most important compensable factors are usually education, expertise, and experience. The important thing is to start. The best compensable factor you have right now is *effort*. You can work hard. Boom!!! Good answer. Whether you are going to work in a salon or in a body shop, working hard gets you on the right path (or staircase or ladder) up your ***Pyramid.***

Compensation (Pay)

How much you can make depends on quite a few things, as you see in the Table 3.4. It also depends on when and where you can work. If this is your starting job, and you are looking to get into the workforce part time, you may not want to spend an hour getting to a job that is only a four-hour shift. Let's scope out some of the factors for your first job in Table 3.5.

Table 3.5 – When, Where, and How Much

How far Away Can I Work

Miles to Work	1	3	5	7	10+
Available Transportation:					
Walk	Yes		No		
Bike/Skate/Scooter	Yes		No		
Public Transportation	Yes		No		
Car	Yes		No		
Hours	Full-Time		Part-Time		
Work Times					
Morning	Yes		No		
Afternoon	Yes		No		
Evening	Yes		No		
Graveyard	Yes		No		
Weekdays	Yes		No		
Weekends	Yes		No		
Shift Work	Yes		No		
Pay Expectations					
	Wage		Salary		
Minimum Wage	_____	$/hr			
Wage Range	_____	$/hr	_____	$/hr	
Union	Yes		No		
Non-Union	Yes		No		
Salary Range	_____	$/month	_____	$/month	

Here is some simple math:

1. Full-time work means you work forty hours in a calendar week—five days at eight hours per day.

2. Your state has a minimum hourly wage that employers must pay you, by law. This varies by state and is loosely related to the cost of living in your state (Google it). You do not want to live forever on minimum wage.

3. Part-time work is anything less than forty hours in a calendar week.

4. There are 2,080 regular working hours in a calendar year (52 weeks × 40 hours per week = 2,080 hours).

5. Some people are paid *hourly*, which means they are paid for each hour they work. Some are paid a *salary*, which means they are paid for a work period, like a month. Managers and more senior-level workers are generally paid a salary. A salary is generally not eligible for overtime.

6. Overtime is extra money paid for working extra—that is, working more than an eight-hour shift or more than five days in a week, or working on a holiday. Rules vary by state.

7. We often estimate 4.3 work weeks in a month and 173 work hours in a month. These are estimates but are close enough to determine how much you are being paid. If you receive a salary of forty thousand dollars per year, that is $3,333 per month or $19.23 per hour—although this fluctuates because some months have more days in them (yay, February).

8. The governments (federal and state) deduct money from your paycheck. Your total pay is referred to as your *gross* pay. How much is deducted depends on what state you live in. You get to keep about 60 to 70 percent of your pay. This is referred to as your *net* pay.

Gross Pay - Income Deductions = Net Pay

9. Some jobs pay *commission*. This is often in sales. This means some or all of your income is based on selling something (like real estate agents who sell homes). Commissioned salespeople receive a percentage of sales (maybe 3 to 5 percent), but they make zero if there are no sales.

10. Some jobs have *bonuses*, which are based on the company doing well. Bonuses can be company-wide, or they can be merit-based, where they are only paid to employees who work exceptionally hard.

11. Increases in pay are based on two factors:

    COLA – Cost of living allowance, which is received by all employees. In the last twenty years, COLA increases have ranged from 0.5 to 3.0 percent of current pay.

    Merit – This is an increase in pay for becoming better at your job. It is based on your performance and helping the company do better, as well as learning more and taking on more responsibility.

Increases in pay are smaller than you think,
and are much more valuable than you know.

It is important to think about where you can work, and you should have some idea of how much you can make right now. We will talk about what you do with the money you make when we talk about your Pyramid in ***Chapter 5***.

Who Will You Be When You Grow Up?

You should jot down a couple of thoughts on where you see yourself with respect to your work career in the future. Life can take us on an interesting journey. Remember, the goal is to be successful, which we will measure by being far from harm, hunger, and homelessness. For us and for our family. In Table 3.6, write down a short message for you to read in ten years.

Table 3.6 – What Job Do You Want

_____

_____

_____

_____

_____

_____

Your Success

Can you be successful?

Circle one.

Yes   No

If you can be successful, then we should start now. Success is a lot of little steps, so keep reading. You are doing well. This is worth your time, and it will pay you back. Hugely. When you get to the end, you will have a good plan and you will realize which of your skills are the important ones.

You

Let's start with you. Let's start with your face, because that is generally the first thing people are going to see when they meet you in person.

Find a mirror. Go into the bathroom if you need some privacy. You probably spend a bunch of time in there anyhow. No one is going to notice. What's one more hour? Let's have a look. Let's consider six parts of your face.

Let's start with your nose. Big, small, crooked? Some say there are six types of noses, some say fourteen. Does it look like a celebrity nose? Do we care? Does it really matter? In the workplace, does it really matter?

Let's check out the forehead, the hairline, your cheekbones, your chin. All of those things that make you, you. Companies have a bunch of parts, too. The parts make the company whole, and they all contribute in their own ways. You and the company that you will end up working for are both living things.

Are your ears sticking out? Is there anything special about your ears? Do they work? No, really. Think about that. Do they work? Are you a good listener? Can people tell if you use them? Think about that.

What about your mouth? Do you show your teeth? How about your smile? How many types of smiles do you have? Do you grin with your lips closed? Laugh with your head back? Do you have a crooked smile? Intense grin? How important is that smile? Do you laugh louder than anyone in the room, or do you not laugh at all because you do not want people to know what you are thinking, or you do not want to show weakness? (Being *Mean*, which we will get to shortly, says you might want to be somewhere in the middle.)

Do you have special eyes? Do you wear glasses, contacts, or shades? Do you squint when you look at people? Do you realize you squint when you either don't like something or you're scared of something? Do you realize that you open your eyes more when you like something (think of the hottie in the coffee shop)? When you like someone, or something, you open your eyes and you raise your eyebrows slightly. If you don't like something, or it bothers you, you close your eyes slightly. Consider that when you meet someone.

Do you think people see you as being trustworthy? Reliable? Strong? Calm?

You can rate yourself in Table 3.7. Then go to Figure 3.1 and put a circle where you think you are when you are on your 1-8 scale. You can slide along the scale depending on the situation. Each situation can be different, maybe sometimes a 3 is required, and sometimes a 7. You can figure out if you might be overdoing or underdoing some of the items in Table 3.7.

Table 3.7 – Self-Assessment

	If a 1 is	If an 8 is	What do you score yourself between 1 and 8
Smile	No smile, small grin	Wide-open mouth smile	
Laugh	Small chuckle	Loud cackle	
Face at rest	Grimace (RBF)[11]	Big smile	
Eyes	Squint	Huge	
Trustworthy	Accepting	Cunning	
Strength	Weak, submissive	Angry, dangerous	
Reliable	Evasive	Intrusive	
Calm	Sleepy	Intense	

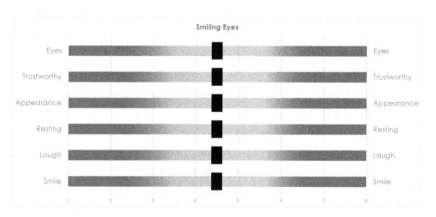

Figure 3.1 – Smiling Eyes Assessment

You should be able to get a good feel for where you want to be. Somewhere in the middle—to start. You should be trustworthy, credible, and reliable. We will come back to that when we meet *Ari* in Chapter 4, where he teaches us how to act *Golden*.

---

11   RBF - Resting bitch face—try to avoid that.

Now that we have looked at ourselves and realize that what we got is what we got, what is going to happen when we walk into a job interview? Or when we start our first day on the job?

Meet the Judge

Turns out, it is pretty simple. People are going to judge you—fast. Fact. And as soon as you see them, you are going to judge them—fast. Fact. We will dive into this a little later, but since you want to get going on the whole job/career thing, I thought we should bring this out in the open now. You are going to meet people in the workplace, and you will judge each other.

We have an evolutionary history of judging the safety of our surroundings. "Oh wow, that is a saber-toothed tiger. I think I better get out of here." There is not a lot of time humming and whistling while you think about it. Those who took a lot of time to think about busting butt getting away from the saber-tooth didn't last very long, so they didn't have much nooky, and thus they left behind no slow-thinking ancestors. After about 7,500 generations of weeding out the slow and the dim-witted, we are left with us quick-thinking speed-rockets. We haven't turned it off. Every one of us is pre-wired to judge people and situations within a fraction of a second. Not "like"/ "don't like." We judge on safety and trust. Not much different than the saber-toothed tiger. Are these people trustworthy, and am I safe being around them? "Oh look, a saber-toothed tiger! Awwwwwww. Should I pet it?"

You can use this to your advantage in school and in the workplace. How about looking safe and trustworthy? After your shift at work, you can go back to your dark room and put on your Sith robe. If you want people to accept you in the workplace, try engaging with them. Here are some tips:

Eyes

Don't squint. We don't trust people who squint. Think about it. When you are around someone you really don't care for and you are forced to interact with them, you likely squint. Keep your eyes open and look people in the eyes. It also helps to raise your eyebrows a bit. Think about baristas at a coffee shop. Do they squint at you, or do they open their eyes a bit wider and raise their eyebrows? Think about grumpy servers. Do they have their eyes open? Take some time to walk around and take a look at people and their eyes.

Smile

Not a great big, wide-open, mind-boggling smile. A small smile. Probably not an open-mouth smile. Just use your Zygomaticus muscle. That is the muscle that brings the corner of your mouth upward and outward. Do you know any frowny faces that seem to be in a downturned perma-frown? It took a while to get that way. A cranky store clerk, a janitor, someone in your family?[12] Don't do that.

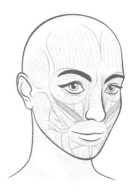

Zygomaticus Muscle

Engage

Everyone you meet is important. Look at their eyes, say "Hi," listen to them, smile (small). Ask them how their day is. Listen to their answer, wish something good for them. "Cool. Have a great day."

---

12   If you want to practice your smile, hold a pen or pencil in your mouth (crossways). That will work your zygomaticus muscle. It is also shown to make you happier, and you perform better.

The Art of a Handshake

Look people in the eye, smile, nod, handshake firm but not crushing. Take your time.

You want to appear trustworthy and respectful to people above and below you. It is a sign of equality. You want to accept the harmony of the workplace that **Org** *is hoping for.*

Some cultures use different forms of greeting, and you never know when you are going to run into someone who wants to hug, bow, or air kiss. Some women are very reluctant to be touched and that is their right. Smile and nod, try to make a connection.

The handshake doesn't have to be too long, but I generally let the other person determine that. Sometimes they seem to hang on because they want to have your attention while someone else speaks.

Kleenex in the pocket is great for absorbing a bit of clamminess if your palms are a bit sweaty. Running your fingers through your hair, if you have any, is another way to dry your hands a bit more.

In the workplace, you are not bros or sports teammates. The traditional style.

I would suggest practicing on family and friends. Male and female. Learn the difference between both men and women, young and old. Better to work with a range of people, rather than just one person.

You should shake hands with a woman the same way you would shake hands with a man. No dead, limp fish. Women in the workplace are equals and just as strong as men.

Also, as people seem to worry more and more about germs and stuff, there are more fist bumps. It might take you off-guard. Try to take a little more time with that person and hold their eyes a little longer to make the connection.

There is more concern about the appropriateness of touching and hugging. Hugging has totally gone out of style at work—unless it is someone you are really close to. Handshake, fist bump, eye contact, smile. This is where you live.

Be Yourself

If you're a little nervous, let people know. Even if it is just talking to a receptionist. It can defuse your nerves and it makes a connection. You would be surprised how often the first person you meet (we call them the "gatekeeper") is asked their impressions of the job candidates. And this holds for all the people you meet, even a senior manager, a vice-president, or the CEO big cheese. Here is a little secret: They are a bit nervous about meeting you. They don't want to screw up and embarrass themselves or you. Cut people some slack.

Pull It All Together

This takes practice. Start from sitting on the couch, make eye contact, smile, stand up, shake hands, say "Hi," ask "How is your day?" Practice at home, or church, or school.

People will judge you.
Make it easy for them to judge you as safe, trustworthy, and reliable.

Package it up, and it's you. That is what you have to offer. It is the biggest part. It is the most important part, and you can be great at it. We will even teach you to be **Golden** at it. You can practice with your family, you can practice with your church, you can practice with your teacher.

Church is a great place to go to practice being trustworthy and safe. You can go and they will accept you. Or try a library, a bookstore, or a shoe store. Just go in and say "Hi." "No, thanks. Just looking. How is your day going?" Safe, reliable, and trustworthy.

Summary

If you are ready to get a job, you are ready. If you are not, we have laid out what you need to do. You will need to gather your information and get it ready so that you have it on hand when you create a resume and fill out job applications. You can give some thought to the type of job you will consider. You are not making a huge decision about the rest of your life. You are just starting to get some work experience and build your resume, get some skills, get some money, and try out adulthood. It's kind of like working out, you may try yoga and decide you are more of a cross-fit type of person. No problem, the yoga wasn't a waste. You may start out with a job in fast food, but decide you are more of an office person, or maybe a warehouse person. No problem. The first job was more valuable than you think.

You are your best asset. Practice your ability to smile and to generate a feeling of safety and trustworthiness. Practice your empathy and kindness, as well as your confidence in your ability to work and to help people. That spark at your core is enough to get you started. You get to build the you that you want to be, which might be a *M.E.*[13] Now we can help you give you some more skills that will help you on your journey.

---

13   Which is you, not me.

CHAPTER 4

Getting to Ari

Beyond the idea of getting a job, entering the workforce, and being successful, where do you start? How are you going to act when you start your new job? How do you become successful? Things are easier if you know they are going to be successful. Good news. You are going to be successful. We are going to build the foundation for your **Pyramid**. Your foundation is going to guide you through the right behaviors for your new job, and Aristotle is going to help. Once you build your foundation no one can take it away from you. It's yours.

Who are those people you see that just seem to have their s*** together? Who are those people that seem to know how to fit into a room, or are able of talking to a new person or a person in authority, like a boss or a cop? How do they talk to the hottie with the hair? What is the skill required to do that? It is a series of skills, and they can be learned.

> From *A Gentleman in Moscow*:
> "... if one did not master one's circumstances, one was bound to be mastered by them ..."
>
> —Amor Towles

We are going to learn how to apply them in the workplace. These are skills we want to master so that we are in control of most situations. We have a rock-solid way to handle those new situations, those new people. But first, let's talk about work and the workplace.

Work

Work (as in selling your skills and your labor) has been around for a long time, but not forever. Sweeping up the cave, skinning the saber-tooth—that goes back a long way. Workplaces have been around a long time, but not forever. Success in the workplace is still a work in progress. Everyone is still trying to figure it out. You are not standing at a party where everyone knows the words to a hit song and you don't. You are not the only one. The only ones who know the words are the ones who have learned the words. Let's learn them. The workplace, like our country, is evolving and changing. Hit songs change with time. Like our country, we can evolve and change and become really good so we come out on top. Respected, esteemed, valued, and well-regarded. It will be *Normal*,[14] and it will be great.

Let's start by looking at how long some things have been around. One hundred years sounds like a long time, but that is when your parent's great-grandparents were your age. It is about five generations. Lots has changed in one hundred years. Things evolve slowly, but always evolve. Usually for the better, although rarely perfectly. Great new things are great, but then they have to get better. Sometimes, great new things are not great for a while, and it can take a generation or two to knock the bugs out of them. We need your help. Table 4.1 presents roughly how many generations things have been around. We will chat about it afterwards. Sorry if the table is a little long—not sorry.

Table 4.1 – History of the World - In Generations

Years Ago	Event	How Many Generations Ago (approximately)	Comments/Notes
14,000,000,000 (fourteen billion)	Origin of the universe.	A bunch	
4,000,000,000 (four billion)	Earth is formed.	Less than a bunch, but a whole lot	
200,000 (two hundred thousand)	Humans appear.	7,500	This is according to scientists (anthropologists) who study what makes us distinctly human.
11,700	Last Ice Age ends; oceans rise 300 feet around the Mediterranean.	480	Sometimes Earth is bigger than us. Earth warmed up without us reducing emissions or using paper straws.

---

14   "Patience, Iago." We are going to work on being *Golden* first. We will learn how *Normal* everything is in Chapter 7. Iago. You know—the parrot from Aladdin.

Years Ago	Event	How Many Generations Ago (approximately)	Comments/Notes
11,000	Agriculture begins to take root in the Mediterranean area, as long, dry summers start to occur, which favor annual plants (grains) that grow, mature, and die in the summer, leaving a dormant seed that can be stored and eaten.	Close to 480	Excess food allowed our ancestors to start to trade other things for food. Maybe you made a cool chair and you could trade that for a bushel of grain. Or maybe you made a really cool pot or vase. Maybe you made a vat of wine from grapes or a barrel of beer from excess grain.
11,000	First permanent settlement around Jericho (what is now the West Bank in Palestine).	About 480	
6,500	City of Uruk, in what is now Iraq, considered the oldest city in the world, home of *Gilgamesh*, the oldest surviving work of literature.	260	People started recording history. They wrote things down to keep track of things like taxes and marriages.
5,000	Pyramids of Egypt are built.	200	
5,000 – 2,000	Egyptian Era	100–200-ish	
3,000 – 1,500	Greek Era	60–120	Wealthy families in cities began getting private teachers for their children. Workers received wages in weight of grain per day.
2,500	The life of Socrates.	100-ish	One of the founders of Western thought; teacher of Plato.
2,450	The life of Plato.	Still 100-ish	Teacher of Aristotle.

Years Ago	Event	How Many Generations Ago (approximately)	Comments/Notes
2,400	The life of Aristotle.	Still 100-ish (we are estimating)	Teacher of Alexander the Great; thinks about how to live the good life. We call him **Ari**, 'cuz he is so cool.
2,000 – 1,500	Roman Era	60–80	
1,500 – 500	Dark and Medieval Eras	20–60	Work was done in the home. It was craft-manship. Trade was mostly local. People could be mean, and it could be dangerous. Healthcare was less than ideal.
500	Reformation	20	There was a break from the Catholic Church. "Protestant[15] work ethic" was thought to have its genesis in the belief that hard work is good for you and your soul. And coffee appeared. Yay, coffee.
250	Industrial Revolution	10	Brought in new materials, energy, machines, work systems, transportation, communication, and mass production. And lots of pollution.
140	Hydrocarbon fuel vehicles invented.	6	Cars started to appear in the 1880s in Europe and North America.
75	Transistor invented.	3	Allowed for the development of computers.

---

15   You know there is a word in Protestant—they were protesting. They became Protestant. They didn't wreck stuff though. They believed in something, they sought it out, and they overcame.

Years Ago	Event	How Many Generations Ago (approximately)	Comments/Notes
70	Smog and pollution overwhelm London and Los Angeles (from 1950-1970).	3	Humans have always had a desire to improve their lives. Protests not always needed. People will support improving the human condition. It might take a while.
			In 1970, new regulations were put into place limiting harmful chemicals from factory smokestacks and from the tailpipes of cars and trucks.
			The regulations have been updated several times to make them more stringent and to make cars and factories cleaner and safer.
30	World Wide Web	Your parents	The rest of this table shows all the technologies that have arrived in your parents' lifetime—and note how long it takes your parents to figure out how to use a new app. Or consider your grandparents.
25	Google	1	
20	Wi-Fi	1	
15	YouTube	1	
13	iPhone	1	
10	iPad	1	
5	Apple Watch	1	

This is not a history text. We created Table 4.1 to show you "us" in a bigger picture. Humans evolved about two hundred thousand years ago. That is about 7,500 generations ago. It took 7,494 generations to figure out the car and the gas-powered engine. We still can't figure out how to cure the common cold or how to put the lid on the toothpaste. We are still a work in progress. Cars were not very fuel-efficient, and it didn't take that many cars to make a lot of pollution. The modern workplace, with centralized factories and standardized pay, is less than ten generations old. We are all still figuring it out so it's safe and fair. We are becoming more efficient and polluting less. We are more responsive and more team-oriented. Managers are generally trying to give people the biggest raises[16] they can. Today's world is intensely competitive, and we need profits to design better, more-sustainable products; build better workplaces; and increase how much we are all paid. The dollars used to pay our wages have to come from somewhere. The dollars to pay taxes have to come from somewhere.

The point is, you are coming into a workplace that is a work in progress. Human civilization is a work in progress. The good thing is that no one is expecting you to be perfect. The great thing is that you can help, you can contribute, you can make it better. Don't get mad at people for the workplace not being perfect; everyone is working on it. Except for the slackasses. But no one likes them.

Perfection

Have you ever noticed that when you start something you don't do it perfectly? Like when you tried dance lessons, or baseball or piano or baking a cake for the first time? You are not perfect at the start and that is *Normal*. You are not going to be perfect when you start your job in the workplace. Agreed. And it is okay.

But we can give you a way to start at your new job and make sure you are on your way to Happyland at work. Let's go back in Table 4.1 to about

---

16   Raises are smaller than you think and more valuable than you know.

one hundred generations ago. Let's go back to the Greeks and take a closer look at our guy Aristotle. He is going to help us lay the foundation for our *Pyramid*. He is going to teach us how to start out. We are going to go back to the beginning to understand how we should begin.

Cuneiform was the first form of writing. It originated around 3400 BC in Mesopotamia (now Iraq) as a way to record records of goods and services—like who owned what cow.

Cuneiform was mostly inscribed onto clay tablets, which were kinda hard to put in your toga pocket.

Hieroglyphics came into play around 3000 BC in Egypt, where the pictures were simplified to represent certain sounds. Aristotle wrote in Greek and Latin.

Papyrus, which came before paper, came from the region around the Nile. It was also used as a source of food, as well as to make shoes, rope, toys, and even small boats. Even one hundred generations ago.

The Greeks gave us more than just a great salad. Sadly, a lot of what they wrote down has been lost—but a lot has survived. The Greeks had some of the first really smart teachers, starting with Socrates, who started thinking about humans doing the right things, and about morals and justice. He wanted people to question things and to think for themselves. Great start.

Socrates taught his students to question their morals, beliefs, and principles. This got him in trouble with the government because the government was worried the students would start to question them. They charged him with "corrupting the young" and with "impiety." The dealio back then was that the (male) citizen jurors found him guilty and voted that he be executed. Because they were such super nice guys, they let him choose how he would die. He chose a poisonous tea made from hemlock, a poisonous flower. The poison killed him. OK. Not a great start.

Before he died, Socrates was a teacher, and he had a student named Plato. Plato learned from Socrates and then founded his own school near Athens, generally referred to as the Academy. You can still visit the Academy for free. It was discovered under a neighborhood a couple of miles from downtown Athens. The school was an enclosed olive grove where students came for free and discussed problems. It is thought at least two women attended as well. The idea behind the Academy was to learn how to think. Plato had a student named Aristotle. Here is our man, born about ninety-five to one hundred generations ago.

Aristotle

Ari studied at Plato's Academy for twenty years (where smart people had cool thoughts—pre-Starbucks, pre-coffee, pre-Internet, and they didn't even have Snapchat).[17] *Ari* was a bright dude and is credited with contributing a lot of things that are still accepted today. He is thought of as a founding father of Western philosophy, although back then he contributed to many areas, including zoology, biology, and other natural sciences.

The big pyramids in Egypt were two thousand years old when Aristotle came along. They were seven hundred miles away from where he grew up, and he couldn't exactly take a plane across the Mediterranean to see them. He is going to help us lay the foundation for your **Pyramid**.

We are going to build your **Pyramid**, and you are going to be responsible for caring for it. Your **Pyramid** will have more of a personal touch. Your **Pyramid** will last your lifetime. Guaranteed. You will build on top of the foundation *Ari* will construct for you.

After learning from Plato, Aristotle started his own school called the Lyceum (which started in a gymnasium). He thought a lot about living the *good life*, and although acceptable behavior has changed in one hundred generations, we can still capture the essence of living the good life. Pretty safe to say we all want to live a good life. *Ari's* main thought was that we should all try to live a good life and try to be good at being a good person.

Ari must have been cool. He tutored a kid who became Alexander the Great (Alexander was the king's kid, and eventually Alexander went around kicking everyone's butt, expanding the Greek empire, and being called "Great"). *Ari* held his school while he walked around and talked to the students who walked behind him. He didn't wear a toga, but he wore a himation, which is pre-toga—definitely fashionable back in the

---

17   Plato's Academy is considered the first school of higher learning (university) of the Western world.

day. He could recite the fifteen thousand-line poem, Homer's *Iliad*, from memory. The *Iliad* was a definite bestseller. See what you can do when there is nothing fun to distract you?

Ari believed the only way you could live a good life was to do good things. If you do good things, good things will happen. And the way to learn how to do good things was to watch and learn how others do good things, and then copy them. .

Find someone who does good things and copy how they act.[18]

Ari called these people who did good things and seemed to have everything figured out *Moral Exemplars*. Bam!!! There it is. There is your *M.E.* You watch and learn from *Moral Exemplars* and let their habits become your habits, and then you will be able to be as good as they are, or eventually you can improve upon them. These are the people that seem really good at things, like the whole talking-to-the-boss or hot-guy/girl thing. It ain't easy. We practice singing like Rihanna, shooting hoops like Curry, and speaking like your favorite teacher. This may seem fake. It is. A bit. Faking to fake out people and do bad things is bad. Faking to learn and to practice and to make yourself better is okay. You will still be you when Gramma comes to visit and squeezes your cute cheeks. That won't change.

Finding Your M.E.

There was no Internet, social media, TV, Hollywood, or rap videos one hundred generations ago. *Ari* and his dudes and dudettes didn't get exposed to a whole lot of people, since you didn't travel that far from home (unless you were in the army and you got into wars and stuff). That probably had a downside. People had to learn from who was around nearby, who had their &*%$ together. Hmmm. Sounds like a good idea today. You probably have someone you admire close by. I hope you do.

---

18   Really, we are saying learn from them. Copy is quicker to type. I am faking it a bit.

The people you choose as your *Moral Exemplars* need to be worthy of your admiration. They are probably not celebrities. We are talking good people in your community. People who are real. Maybe just a regular good person in your life. These are the people who will help you in the workplace. In Table 4.2, let's make a list of some *M.E.* characteristics you think people should have to be worthy of being your *M.E.* A few are listed just to get you going. Then list some candidates who might be worthy of your admiration and who you might want to learn from, and you can copy some of their behaviors.

Table 4.2 – Moral Exemplars: Characteristics & Candidates

Moral Exemplar Characteristics		
Kind		
Smart		
Strong		
Moral Exemplars Candidates		

Ari thought that what makes us different from animals is our ability to reason. To think. To know right from wrong. Ari believed that building character in important areas such as courage (being strong in life), temperance (not getting loaded every night), subject expertise (knowing a lot about something that matters), and generosity (helping out others) was important. Building character is done by learning and making characteristics into habits. Repeat after me. Habit. Repeat. (That is a habit.)

We really need to think of the characteristics we take into the workplace. You do not need to be college educated to be a great person, a great worker, a great co-worker, or an *M.E.* Give this some thought and look for your *Moral Exemplars* that will help you in the workplace.

The Golden Mean

This is hugely important! You don't have to be perfect, especially at the start. *Ari* believed that in each of the **Moral Exemplar** characteristics (kind, smart, strong, etc.) you should start out somewhere in the middle. You don't want to start at the extremes. You don't need to start way out there, or way up at the top. If the characteristic is *courage*, you don't want to be so courageous you run out in front of a bullet or get your ass kicked by someone clearly stronger and tougher than you. What purpose would that serve? You also don't want to run and hide. How about you go get an authority figure who can deal with Buttwad? How about you stand up for what is right? In the adult world, that is fine. Getting your ass kicked by someone a hundred pounds heavier and six inches taller doesn't do anything for you or the situation you are trying to help.

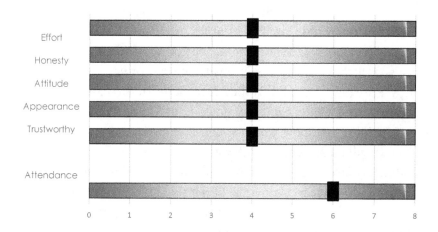

Figure 4.1 Golden Mean - The Start

If we are talking about *generosity* as a characteristic, you are not helping anyone by buying a drug addict drugs, or by donating your rent check to a puppy shelter. You should do something to help others with your good fortune, but the help needs to help without hurting you or them. Then you are generous.

This idea is what is referred to as Ari's **Doctrine of the Golden Mean.** (This is *Mean* in the mathematical sense—an average—not being mean to your little sister. *Come on, what were you thinking*!?!)

Ari's idea was that a good life was lived between extremes.

You don't have to be the ultimate best at everything, most popular, best looking, fastest, strongest, smartest, craziest, skinniest, funniest, angriest, most liked, or most followed. It should be easy to see that you cannot live a good life doing nothing. You gotta put yourself out there—some. You can learn to operate by being in the middle and doing good. And you can help a lot, and that is what we are setting out to do. Remember, we need your help. Average, in the middle, *Mean* is a great start.

The Mean Behaviors

Table 4.3 describes some behaviors for the workplace. I have left plenty of room for you to add your own ideas for behaviors at work and in your personal life. Cool. Go for it. You may see things differently. Our main focus is work, but you can apply this to the rest of what you do if you want. We are going to call this the *Mean Table.* In this case, the desired behavior is between deficient (not enough) and excessive (too much). If we get it right, then how we act is considered virtuous—bonus points for you! It will make people think you are Baden-ass—I was hoping for a moderately amusing thing to write down. Kind of average, which in this case would make it *Mean.* It is similar to Baden-ess, but I have never been to Baden-Baden, which we mentioned when we got relative.[19] Not hilarious, not offensive—maybe mildly amusing.

---

19   If this seems confusing, go to the discussion of the Müller-Lyon Illusion in Chapter 1.

This is an example of humor that is **Mean**. Certainly not great. Hopefully not awful. **Mean** at best. I am okay with that.

Table 4.3 – The Mean Table

Behavior	Deficient (too little)	Virtue (mean)	Excessive (too much)
Effort	Lazy	Engaged	Reckless
Cooperative	Goofs off	Contributes	Distracting
Truthful	Omits	Honest	Lies
Company resources (supplies)	Steals	Respects	Wastes
Company $	Gives away	Understands	Wastes
Attitude	Absent	Positive	Hostile
Appearance	Slob	Professional	Inappropriate
Training	Doesn't care	Learns	Already knows everything about everything
Safety	Ignores	Respects	Hypersafe
Helpful	Absent	Attentive	Overbearing
Respect	Ignorant	Appreciative	Faking
Communication	Silent	Engaged	Will not shut up
Knowledge	Silent	Converses and listens to other thoughts and ideas	Knows absolutely everything about everything

One thing that should jump out from Table 4.3 is that certain characteristics fit different behaviors. Maybe you can think of different or better words. Go for it, that is okay. We all learn from each other, and every situation is different. This is kind of like you starting your job. You might not be an expert, or experienced—but you have a lot to add. Go ahead and fill in the table with your thoughts on the right behavior. Everyone is looking for input, or new ideas. Except for Buttwads. Buttwads don't add anything. Hopefully, Buttwads are the exception rather than the rule.

It should also pop out at you that not every situation desires the exact average of deficiency and excess. Sometimes you want to be closer to excess, sometimes closer to deficient. If you are working in a library, you may want to back off and let people find their way. It's a little quieter. Assist when asked; library people probably like their space. If you are working in a store where us poor old dads are trying to buy a birthday gift for their young adult and we have a bewildered look on our face—HHEEEELLLLLPPPPP! Each situation has its own set of behaviors. If you can start in the middle and then adjust from there, you might be better off than being overly deficient or excessive. We need your help.

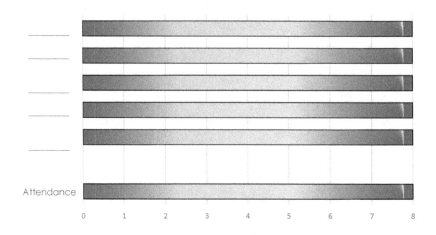

Figure 4.2 – Your Mean Chart

We can chart out our behavior and keep track of whether we acted deficiently or excessively, or if we have our *Mean* on. Maybe we use a eight-point scale like in Figure 4.1, and we can assess how we are doing on a day-to-day basis. Pick out your five important characteristics and consider how you might try to be average, and then move in the right direction along the line. I have included my characteristics in Figure 4.3, so you can use it as a guide. Note there is no average on attendance. You need to show up. Always. A funeral may be an excuse to miss work, but only if you book the day off. You never, ever just not show up!

The *Golden Mean* is a good recipe for young adult life. For the *Mean Table*, we took Aristotle's *Doctrine of the Golden Mean* and updated it. If you can be successful at the whole *Golden-Meanie* thing, you are considered *Virtuous*. Aristotle defined *virtue* as the tendency to behave in the right manner—you want to do right and you *do* do right (as opposed to knowing, and not doing, or worse, getting pleasure from not doing right). Note that he didn't say one way of acting or behaving was right, and another was wrong. He put out some guidelines that kinda make sense, like making choices between not enough (deficient) and too much (excess). *Ari* was a philosopher, but he believed you didn't make the right decision by sitting on a rock each time you had to make a decision. You learn by doing. He thought it was best to develop some good habits. He saw life as more learning through practice. I think he was spot on.

> We have to emphasize timeliness and attendance. You have to show up, and you have to be on time. If you don't show up, you are letting everyone down who has to cover for you. If you are always late, you look like you think you are more important than the people you work with. Expect people to judge you on that.

The Author

Figure 4.2 is my personal Old Guy Chart for Business. This is me when I am consciously trying my best (most of the time). This is how I approach each day at work.

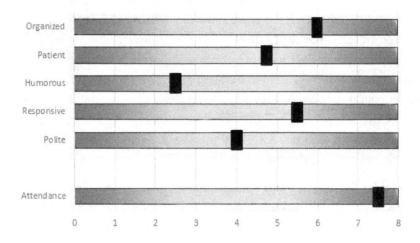

Figure 4.3 – Author's Mean Chart

I try to give a lot to what I am doing and try to be as honest as I can realistically be with people. I maintain a positive attitude, glass always three-quarters full. I work in a fairly casual industry, but I always wear ironed, long-sleeve shirts and black jeans. No flashy name brands. I put a little extra money into my shoes. If I am going to be speaking to a group or presenting at a conference or a seminar, I will wear a sport jacket. If I am in the Caribbean, I am more likely to wear a suit and tie, because it is important to them. Hopefully, I am seen as trustworthy. I always show up on time or just a few minutes early.

How does my behavior chart compare to yours? Does it matter if you are working in an office, a store, a salon, or a body shop? The behaviors that will move you up in the company and gain respect are usually about the same.

Workplace Habits

Finding your way through that first job will take practice, and you will not be perfect. You also will not be at that first job for the rest of your life. Getting that first job—whatever it is—will certainly put you on a path for a *Normal* chance of success or a *Normal* chance of failure. Life is *Normal*.[20]

The good habits you develop in the workplace can be really small at first, but they can make you stand out in the workplace. Table 4.4 offers some simple workplace examples.

Table 4.4 – Mean Work Habits

Characteristic	Habit	Description
Reliable	Timeliness	You do not have to show up an hour early, but you definitely cannot be late. You need to be reliable. It might mean leaving a party early to get home to get enough sleep.[21] You need to be *ready to work* at the appointed time—not showing up and running through the door at the appointed time. You need to be at your station, desk, area, with your tools, pen, paper, plan, wrenches, vacuum cleaner, personal protective equipment (PPE). Ready to go.
Communication	Greetings	Smile and greet most people most of the time when you see them. Greeting and hugging everyone every time might be overcooking it. A positive small smile, like you are enjoying your day, goes a long way.
Cleanliness	Clean up your room— or, uh, your workplace	When you meet **Org**[22] you are going to feel bad for the dude. **Org** has a lot going on, and certainly doesn't have time or money to hire a maid to look after you. Keep your workplace neat and tidy. Clean it up every day. Organize your work tools, your thoughts, and your goals for each shift at the beginning of each shift. Make cleaning up easy by always cleaning up.

---

20   Chapter 7. Be patient.

21   Nothing good happens after midnight, especially if you are trying to keep away from harm, hunger, and homelessness.

22   You are going to meet *Org* in Chapter 10.

Characteristic	Habit	Description
Cleanliness	Clean the coffee room breakroom	There is likely no maid or full-time coffee room attendant to clean it up every day. If you are the new person and you clean it up—as simple as wiping a counter, throwing trash in the trash, and making fresh coffee when it has been sitting there for hours (even if you don't like coffee)—what people will see is that you are helpful, you are humble, and you make their lives better. Get that thought in their heads and other good things will normally come your way. You want to show other people that you are part of the team, and you do not think you are too good for them, or that you are better than them.
Reliable	Timecards, paperwork	Do it properly, every day and on time. If you are writing anything down—BE NEAT. Even if you have to slow down a bit. Ask if you are doing it right. Do not leave it and hope some other part of **Org**—who likely has way better things to do—will fix it for you.
Cleanliness	Clean up and put everything back when you are done with it	Walk through your workspace (maybe it is a yard, maybe your section of a store) before you leave to catch anything you missed. Put away hoses, rakes, tools; coil up your ropes; pick up the garbage on the ground. In some jobs, people bring their own tools. You need to respect their property. They can be mighty sensitive about some new whippersnapper coming along and taking their screwdriver. Just beware.
Reliable	Do what you say you are going to do	If you say you will have the filing done by Friday, have the filing done by Friday. Or if you say you will fill in the spreadsheet by the end of the day, fill in the spreadsheet by the end of the day. Even if there is a great cat video floating around the office that everyone is watching.
Humble	Ask for help if you need it, say you're sorry if you screw up	No one expects you to know everything, and if you get stuck you can ask for help. It helps if you can laugh at yourself a bit and it helps if you can say "Thank you" for taking them away from what they were doing just to help you.

Characteristic	Habit	Description
Be coachable	Allow people to teach you	No one likes anyone who knows everything.

Again, the table has some empty space left for you to add some of your own thoughts on some good habits, or go ask your parents or some older relatives for input. Add some things that you might be able to do well because you rock at doing them. Maybe it is wiping down tools, organizing your cubicle, or wiping down the coffee room at the start of a shift.

Be a Chef

The great French chefs start each day by planning everything and making a strategy for their meals. Preparing everything and laying out everything they are going to need, getting what they are going to cook, and putting out their supplies, their spices, their accoutrements, so they do not start a dish only to realize they do not have any paprika.[23] For you, it might mean thinking through your day and making sure you have a pen, knowing where the extra roll of receipt tape is, or anticipating what PPE (personal protective equipment) you are going to need for the day.

Ari did pretty well considering the information he had available. The world seemed mysterious back then, and people were trying to make sense of it, just like they are now.[24] They had no university studies or social media, so they got by on common sense. Today, no matter how

---

23 Having no paprika would suck.

24 It may help to note that during ancient Greek times, there were only four substances: earth, fire, water, and air. That is as complicated as it got. Thoughts were being shaped, times were different. But they provided us with a starting point that has advanced and changed through the centuries. Like work is changing.

educated some people get, they don't get the common-sense part. Maybe a couple of case studies on being *Mean* will help us make sense of this.

We learned in Chapter 2 that we judge people automatically, and they judge us. Maybe we should practice getting in the habit of being *Mean*[25] when we judge people. We will not want to screw up by overdoing it and being rude to the boss. We will not want to screw up by ignoring the boss. We will want to be respectful and attentive. Most bosses will be good; that is why they have been chosen to lead people and to represent.

Incomplete Information

You will get a boss at your first job. It is great if you can understand that the boss has a few things in common with a police officer. Both of these people are most likely good, likely not perfect. The boss is trying to figure out what is going on in a business sense; the police officer is working in the social sense. You need to learn how to act around them and communicate with them. It will help move you away from harm, hunger, and homelessness.

Just like you probably do not tell your parents or your teachers everything you do, bosses and police officers are always trying to figure out what is happening or why something happened. Both are capable of making mistakes. They will both fall under our Chapter 7 rule—*Life is Normal.* What kind of behavior will it take to put your best foot forward in speaking to one of these people? How can you make them want to talk to you again? What about when you meet someone else?

---

25 Remember, we mean average, not mean.

Six Things for Meeting People

Cellphone put away	Stand, if appropriate	Open your eyes and smile
Pay attention to them	No side conversations	Listen

Whoever I am going to talk to, I am going to take my hands out of my pockets, and I am going to put my cellphone away. I am going to show respect by paying attention to them. I am not going to have a side chat about the weekend when the boss is there to thank you for the work you did last week. I want to appear trustworthy and reliable. If I am sitting, and the situation seems right, I will stand if I am going to have a conversation with them. If I am meeting my new boss, I am going to try to smile and shake hands, fist bump, bump elbows . . . or just smile and nod. I will open a conversation by asking them how their day is going or acknowledging what is happening ("Thanks for giving me the opportunity" or "The new tools are really helping, who do I thank for that?" or "I am doing some safety training; sounds nuts, but I am looking forward to it"). I am going to be **Mean**. And I am going to be **Golden**.

I am going to open my eyes, make eye contact, and smile. If I am wearing shades, I am going to take them off. I am going to try to not be deficient, and I am going to try not to be excessive. I am going to trust that if I respect them, they will respect me. The question for you to ask yourself is: Which of the **Mean** traits do you have that you can use going into this situation?

Traits I am going to use when I meet someone new:

_____

_____

_____

If you have mostly agreed with most of what you have read so far, then let's consider one more situation before we commit **Mean** to our knowledge toolbox. Many have failed in what we are about to talk about. Being social outside of work is not high school. The workplace is an adult world, and there will be adult activities—team building, bonding, training. This is a great time to start with temperance (in the workplace) and work from there. You do not want to be drunk and stupid the first time you go to the Christmas party.[26] People will remember that behavior for a long time. Let someone else be the ass. You be you. Kind, engaged, smart, strong, and most of all, be respectful.

If all of this has made sense, and you can see how being **Mean** and building character is a good thing and if you can see that you should do mostly good, that you should try to help, and you should do more that builds your character, then you should not do things that harm your character (or your reputation, if you prefer). If you are going to be **Mean**, there are things that you should not do:

- Engage in criminal activities (because then you're hurting someone, even though you might not know them).

- Support organized crime (buying or using illegal drugs). If you are buying or using illegal drugs, you are supporting organizations that participate in more than drugs; they participate in human trafficking, sex slavery, murder, extortion, and more. Do you really want support all those things? Do you really want to be around people who do?

- Wreck stuff. It costs money people don't have if you wreck things, like buildings or parks or schools or bus stops. Or windows. Who breaks windows?

- Make anyone's day a bad day on purpose. Make a boss's day a bad day, or your co-worker's day a bad day, or a police officer's day a bad day. People who do that suck.

---

26 You already know how to not clean up your room. Same skill, different walls. Learn how not to get hammered. Put off being a drunken sot.

Summary

Now we know how to act. We know how we are going to start. This is a simple strategy that involves being ordinary and finding your **M.E.** Start by being average (**Mean**) in the beginning and learn from others, maybe by copying them. Ari's **Golden Mean** is always there for us to choose to not be lacking, nor to be overdoing something. We can learn which things to do in moderation, which things to do a little more, and which to do a little less.

Work as we know it today has been around for quite a while, but not forever. It is always changing and improving. Maybe it is improving slowly, but there are a lot of great people who are trying to make it better, and to make everyone's life better. They just need your help.

Go be **Mean**. Now you have a great foundation.

CHAPTER 5
The Maz

If you come away from this book remembering the **Maz** and your **Pyramid**, then we have done something positive, and our time has not been wasted. The **Maz** teaches us a way to look at others and understand why they may be acting the way they are—your friends, your family, your co-workers. The **Maz** is also a way to look at ourselves and understand a bit about what drives us, what should drive us. The **Maz** is a bit about what we should worry about. It will tell us a lot about how we should handle our **Pennies** (more on that later). A lot of people learn about this in college, but they forget it because they just pay their money, get their degree, and then move on. This will be cheaper and much longer lasting.

Abraham Maslow (the **Maz**) was a psychologist (they study how people act and how they behave) from Brooklyn, New York. Dr. Maslow is recognized as the first psychologist who studied normal people. That's weird. Before that, psychology was mostly about studying the weird, the abnormal, the depraved, and so on. The **Maz** came up with a way of looking at life that has a positive spin, and he put our needs in order. He wanted people to understand they had to satisfy their basic needs first. Then they could try to satisfy their higher (and probably more fun) needs. Instead of being all Shrekian and life having layers, Maz saw life as a series of platforms.

"Gotta have one platform before ya can move up onto the next."

Before life gets good, you have to meet some very basic needs. You ain't no good to nobody if you are naked and got no shoes.

Maslow didn't come from a big Ivy League university and he wasn't born rich. He was born in 1908 in Brooklyn and had six younger brothers and sisters. His parents were Jewish and moved the family to the US. They were fleeing persecution in Russia (which was bullying—with attitude … and guns). The *Maz* grew up experiencing racism from the other kids in New York, and even from his teachers. He didn't get along with his Mom. They didn't have much money. *Maz* spent time lifting weights and hanging out in libraries (sounds *Mean*, sounds *Golden*). Probably a survival instinct. He went to City College of New York, tried law, didn't like it. There was probably some disappointment in that. Then he tried Cornell, but his grades weren't good and it cost too much money. He ended up getting a bachelor's[27] degree from City College and going to the University of Wisconsin, where he got a graduate degree in psychology. But that is all background. The **Maz** didn't pop out of his Mommy's tummy as a genius, and he didn't have gold-tinted diapers or a chauffeur—few people do. The **Maz** didn't quit. Sounds *Normal*. Sounds *Mean*.

The Pyramid

You are going to build your **Pyramid** and your **Pyramid** is going to guide you so you can focus on what you need to focus on. It is going to provide the structure for much of your life and most of your decisions. Your **Pyramid** is going to show you how to make the most out of your money. Paying attention to your Pyramid and paying attention to the right things in the right order is the best way to reduce your stress level, and to make

---

27 A bachelor's degree is generally what you get after attending college for four years and passing all the right classes.

good decisions to avoid harm, hunger, and homelessness. Your **Pyramid** is yours and yours alone.

Figure 5.1 Mazlow's Hierarchy of Needs

In university-smarty-pants circles, Maslow is best-known for his **Hierarchy of Needs** (see Figure 5.1). *Needs* is about potential. For our purposes, let's look at it this way. We all want to be really happy and belong, with great self-esteem, and sit and meditate with a smile on our face and have a puppy that never barks or pees on the floor, but that doesn't happen unless a bunch of other things have happened first. For instance, we need food and we need a place to sleep. If we are hungry, we can't really think about anything else. If we don't have a place to sleep, how we will ever be rested? Most people want some order and structure in their lives. That is why, in the wealthiest country in the world in the late nineteenth century, we installed public service institutions like public schools and police forces. Once we are well-fed and safe, we can worry about belonging, and then we can start to contribute to society and feel good about ourselves. At our peak, we look at reaching our dreams and our goals.

In our lives, we are going to need a very basic foundation to make all this happen. We built the foundation with **Ari's Golden Mean** in the last chapter. Now you are going to build your **Pyramid** on your most excellent foundation.

Things to Consider Before Building Your Pyramid

We live in the United States of America, and most of us are relatively safe. As human beings, our most basic need is to survive. We need clean air, clean water, salt, heat, food, sleep, shelter, sex (eventually—would you please concentrate?). You might want to consider those items for a second. Someone is providing that for you (not the sex, forget the sex, this is not about sex—it's about all the other stuff). Could be parents providing for you, could be one parent, could be a sibling or a relative, could be a foster parent. Whoever it is, they may be really lucky, and not have to really worry about rent or heat or buying groceries. Or they could be worrying about paying bills, making rent, buying food, keeping their job, marriage, paying for gas, and worrying about their own parents' health. Phew. And they are supposed to smile all day long.

It's pretty hard to be all happy and stuff if you are worried about food, heat, shelter, and all that. That is the essence of the **Maz**. Like a house is a structure where you live, your **Pyramid** is the structure of how you live. Like a home is the place where your heart is, the **Maz** is the essence of your life. There are different levels in life that you need to address. Before you can move up to another level of your Pyramid, you have to have a firm grip on the level you are on. You don't get to go straight to the

There is a saying attributed to Isaac Newton: "If I have been great, it is because I have stood on the shoulders of giants." What a great saying. I wish I had said that. But Isaac Newton beat me to it—by four hundred years.

penthouse suite on the top floor. You don't have to be totally finished with one level to move up and try things out on the next level, and you can be happy even if you are on one of the platforms near the ground floor. What you need to be satisfied on one platform may be totally different than what other people, or Hollywood people, or Netflix people, or social media people need. If you don't have a good grip, it is pretty easy to slide down your **Pyramid**—and who knows how far you might slide.

You probably already realize that other people have their own struggles along the way. Remember that teacher, or that boss? They are somewhere in their *Maz,* which can seem like a maze, in a maize field, which could be kinda corny (but spelled incorrectly!). It's pretty straightforward. And a small note: *Maz* never used a pyramid to present his idea; some smart editor or publisher must have done it. Someone came along and made his thoughts better. The *Maz* was a giant whose shoulders we stand on. Everyone can come up with a good idea. And people take good ideas and make them better. Giants and shoulders. You end up knowing that you have to build your *Pyramid.*

The top of the *Pyramid* is not about fame or riches. You don't have to graduate top in your class, get a scholarship, write a hit song, cure cancer, fix your family, and be the world's number one hottie with perfect hair. You don't have to go to college to have a great *Pyramid.* You will learn that climbing the *Pyramid* is about the journey. It is not about celebrity. Celebrities are not necessarily great people. They may be good at something (like looking good, pretending—acting—good, singing or rapping good). Being respected for doing good will be different. Being respected for doing good will add structure and strength to the platforms on your *Pyramid.*

So just like *The Sound of Music* (hey, it's a classic), let's start at the very beginning. We are going to start with the basics. We started with our *Mean* foundation. Now we are going to map out our *Pyramid* and start working our way up. We will figure out how to handle our *Pennies* as we go, so we are always moving away from harm, hunger, and homelessness.

Physiological Needs

It is a big word: physiological. It means biology systems in organisms like us, and how we function in the sciency-biological way. Thanks for sticking with it. A big word like physiological is one of many things we will see that appear to be a little more complicated than they are. Don't get hung up by how many letters there are. Just think sciency-biologically. Think about the most basic things you need. They are not your iPhone, your shoes, or your best friend. You need clean air to breathe, clean water to drink, healthy food to eat. You need heat to stay warm, you need sleep, you need food—or at a most basic level, you need salt. The *Maz* saw sex as a basic human need.

Salt is in your sweat and in your tears. It's in your pee. Salt regulates our muscles and our nerves. Without salt, you cannot regulate the fluids in your body. Eventually bad things happen. Like you die.

Too much salt makes your body hold on to too much water, and that makes your heart have to work harder (high blood pressure).

No wonder people like him. But let's not worry about that right now. This book is about work.

You can likely live three weeks without food, but don't try it. If you have days where you are worried about these seemingly free things, you will pretty quickly learn there isn't much else you can worry about. Again, we are lucky. There are places in the world where these basic needs (like water) are much harder to get. When these basics of human existence are hard to get, they become your reason for existence.

We cannot emphasize this enough. Now or later. Your working life needs to provide food and water, heat and shelter. Your money needs to go there first. And you need to save some for the day when you have no money coming in. Wow, let's say there is a pandemic, and the world shuts down for a few months. You want to control your own destiny—and life will be *Normal*.

The first thing our job does is help us survive, next we work on surviving safely.

Safety

Once you are fed and rested, you need a safe environment. Whether you live in an apartment or a house or a trailer, ceilings keep the rain out, walls keep the heat in (or out, depending where you live). Hopefully, you live in a nice place and you have a window to let some light in. Together the walls, doors, windows, and roof provide a barrier from harm. You may have a yard that provides another little barrier to danger. We have law enforcement to try to keep the bad guys in check. We have rules and regulations that are put in place to stop us from doing dumb things to hurt ourselves (like not wearing a helmet or not wearing a seatbelt). You are going to work to give yourself a level of safety. Bad things can happen anywhere.

In our cities and towns, our safety is based on a *social contract*. It's a term that goes back to the 1760s when smarty-pants like Thomas Hobbes and Jean-Jacques Rousseau started thinking about what made governments legit. In simple terms, we all give up some of our freedoms—to do whatever we want—in exchange for having the benefits of peace and order. The other option is no order, and then everyone gets what they can take, and the strongest can do whatever they want—rape, murder, plunder. Part of the contract says we have police to keep the order and to try to make sure no one gets out of hand and makes the city or town or airport unsafe for others. Law enforcement and the courts are *Normal*, and they help us more than they hurt us. Hopefully, we do our part to help.

There will be lots of rules and regulations about safety in the workplace. No one wants you to break those rules. No one wants you to take the risk. The downside of an accident is always worse than the potential upside of taking a shortcut. No one in a workplace wants you hurt.

If we roll it all together, at some level we work to reduce the risk of harm, hunger, and homelessness. That helps keep us safe.

We also need freedom from fear. It is hard to think about love and belonging when you are scared or living in danger. If you are in danger, can you think of anything but safety? Here is what we can do to do our part. We have a *social contract* with others that says we are going to obey society's rules, and if not, then society's referees—the police and the courts—are going to put us in the penalty box. And since I am following the rules, you should, too. And if you do not follow the rules, I do not have to take matters into my own hands—we have specialists to deal with your issues.

There are all kinds of different places to live—cities, big cities, hot cities, cold cities, small towns, small cities. They all have some basic similarities—good people, bad people, suffering from the heat or the cold, maybe critters that hurt people, or bad people who are critters that hurt people. Usually, the reason you live where you live is because that is where your family is or that is where you work. Makes sense. Moving is hard because it involves risk—it could always be worse. Moving is a big decision we should think about.

We learn to accept our environment and we do not see it in absolute terms, we see it relative to yesterday. Is it better or worse than yesterday? Is it worse than it has ever been? How do we relocate a family with all the jobs, friendships, schools, churches, and teams that are such a huge part of our life? Tough question. Life is full of tough questions.

Absolute measures something against zero. Relative measures something in a comparison to a point of reference. Consider one thousand dollars. It has an absolute value of one thousand dollars. But how you and Jeff Bezos (billionaire) value one thousand dollars is relative. You may value the one thousand dollars more than he does because it changes your situation more than it changes his.

But if the safety of your family is at risk, you might not be able to climb up that **Pyramid** where you are right now. Sometimes we think our family is the only thing we have. Great thought. Lots of families in the world separate for a bit so that someone can go make a better situation and then bring the rest of the family when they are settled. Maybe that can or should be you. There are a lot of reasons why moving to a safer environment can be a good idea. It won't work in every instance. There are a lot of great opportunities out there. Maybe it is up to you. Life will always be **Normal**.

Help us to Safety

You can skip this part, but consider this: If you accept that one of the reasons you want to work is you want to reduce the risk of harm, hunger, and homelessness for you and your family, and if you want more safety in your security platform, then why would you ever do something that brings you closer to harm, hunger, and homelessness? Consider drugs—legal and illegal drugs. You risk your own Pyramid, and you put a lot of stress on the social contract we all have because you are participating in illegal activities, helping fund illegal activities like sex trafficking, illegal guns, and other organized crimes. What do you think the money spent on drugs goes to? Do you think it goes to funding little league and puppy shelters? Our police would love to spend time visiting little league games and handing out traffic tickets, or catching people making out down by the river. Cops are there to protect kids and families, keep people safe, and make sure nasty despicable people are kept from harming cute little sweethearts like you. Just consider that. You protest someone who says or sells something you don't like, but you support the scum of society? Make your own choice. Don't be an ass.[28]

If we take care of some basic human needs, we will have a strong basic human platform to work from. It is fine if you think that worrying about harm, hunger, and homelessness does not apply to you. Congratulations. You are one of the lucky ones. You can stand on your very stable platform, and now you can think about where you belong.

---

28 We have some great ideas on how to avoid supporting the baddies using skills you already have. Keep reading.

Love and Belonging

One of the biggest motivators in our life is to feel like we belong. Belonging is one of the biggest stresses in high school (mostly because our families have taken care of our need for food, shelter, and safety). We all want to feel like we belong. You have been going to school for years. That feeling of going into a new classroom or gym and hoping you see your best friend, or at least a friendly face. It is stressful starting out at a job, but it is great because people want to accept you and make you feel like you belong. They need your help.

We want to contribute and show we are adults.

Belonging is contributing to something bigger than you. Maybe it is smiling and being a little extra nice to your customer as they try to deal with their kid. Maybe you take a couple of seconds to say "Hi" and be a little extra kind to an elderly person. Make them feel a little extra safe. Make them feel you care about them just because they are alive.

It is in people's best interest to be self-interested—interested in what is best for them. Your best friend might get up and move. Might marry someone and be gone or get a whole new set of friends. They may go off to college and never come back. That can be a hardship. It can also be an opportunity. When you enter the workforce, you get a chance to reinvent yourself. You can be a contributor, an asset, a star, an *M.E.* for everybody to see. By being *Mean*, being on the good side of *Normal*, you can get a good slice of the *Pie*. You can belong. You get a work family that loves you.

You can belong at work. You can be part of a team. It's a team that changes over time, but if you are working forty hours a week, and you sleep six hours a day, work is a third of your waking hours. It seems like a good investment to try to belong and feel part of a team. You might be surprised, but when you start a new job, people will reach out to you, and they want to make you part of the team. You are strengthening their team. They are improving their third of their waking hours by having you help them. It is in their own self-interest to make their work life

72

better. It's an opportunity for you to make your life better. You might find this new group is a new world. They will be *Normal*. It sounds kind of exciting, even if a little scary.

Those first days at any job are nerve-racking. It can go on for months. You are going to be on a learning curve, occupying your spot in the *Org*—a new family, a new group, some new friends. As you get to know *Org*, it gets better. Knowing how the *Org* puts itself together will help us understand how to navigate our way through *Org*'s headspace. We will learn about that later.

One day, after you have put yourself out there and given some of yourself to your job, you will find that you belong, and that people care about you. They appreciate you helping them with their work life. You may find it happens sooner than you think. Wow, congratulations, you do belong. Now other people are helping you build the *Pyramid* you just started. It will be *Normal*, but it will be mostly great. We need your help.

Self-Esteem

Self-esteem is the opinion we have of ourselves. It builds on the supporting levels of our *Pyramid*—how well we have done in taking care of our health and safety and how much we feel we belong within our family and our tribe. You can add belonging in the workplace.

During those early days of work, you are the job. It is the job. It is not you. If you feel nervous, or you are asked to deal with the public—be the job. Remember you can be *Mean*—take it. *"Fake like Ari, fake like Ari, you got faayayayayayake it like Ari"* sung to some old Maroon 5 song.

Smile, be friendly, make eye contact, speak so people can understand you. You can go back to being you later, after work. You can go crawl onto your phone or put on your wizard robe. Whatever. On the job, be the job.

People spend a lot of money trying to feel good. The workplace pays you money to feel good. Contributing, helping, being *Golden*, and being your *M.E.*

Remember, this book is about the workplace. It is not focused on your feelings with the rest of your community or your tribe. It is not about your politics or your social justice. It is not about your favorite song. This is not school where everyone should respect each other for no reason and be nice no matter what. This is work. The workplace might be just the place to go to feel good about yourself, and you earn it. When you earn it, no one can take it away from you.

Your self-esteem is going to be a pretty good predictor of how things turn out for you. If you feel pretty good about yourself, you will likely see things in a positive light, and things will seem okay. If you think you suck as a person, then you are likely going to think everything and everyone sucks. If you think this is the case right now, go back and read again about being a *Golden Meanie*, so you don't turn into a *Golden Wienie*.

Self-esteem is how we feel about ourselves—truly, deep down—and how we think others see us—our reputation and how much we are respected. This is where the *Maz* connected the dots. Can you really respect yourself if you cannot provide for yourself? Can you really feel a sense of belonging if you can't throw some money in for pizza or buy your Mom a flower on Mother's Day? (You can write your Mom a card and save the ten dollars. She will think it is great—and you get the self-esteem boost—win! That's *Golden.*)

Can you be proud and have self-respect making minimum wage? Damn right you can, especially if you are *Mean* about it. And if you are *Mean* about it, the minimum wage will be temporary (a few months?), and you will likely end up with a bigger piece of *Pie.*

If you are *Mean* about it, your *Pyramid* will be just fine. Think good, do good. Even in small ways.

Self-Esteem Check

Let's do a quick self-check to make sure everything is okay. Table 5.1 has some words related to how you feel about yourself. You can add some other words if you think they might fit. Then score yourself on eight to ten traits. It is worth it. It will just take a couple of seconds. Score yourself between 1 (weak) and 10 (strong) for each word in Table 5.1. Don't think too much about it. Whatever comes into your mind first.

There are some empty spaces for you to provide your own words. Don't skip them. You need to start doing things and completing things yourself, with your big-person booties on. Count up how many great traits you have and then total up the scores.

Table 5.1 – Self-Esteem Traits

	Score		Score		Score
Confident		Team player		Sharing	
Wise		Tolerant		Organized	
Risk taker		Self-aware		Caretaker	
Independent		Empathetic		Planner	
Trusting		Punctual		Take criticism well	

Number of traits you evaluated (A)   _____

Total score of those traits (B)   _____

Average score (B/A)   _____

How do you feel about the number of good skills and positive traits you have? What do you think you need to work on so that you do okay in the workplace? Maybe Ari had some ideas for you in case you missed them. Learn from someone. Copy someone. Fake it until your esteem is all you.

The workplace is a great place to work on your self-esteem,
and you get paid to do it.

The thing about the workplace is you already know the things you need to know to be successful in the workplace. Those traits you have that are great are also great skills for the workplace.

The purpose of this book is to help you in your first jobs, or during the first part of your career. From the perspective of your self-esteem, we want you to understand two things:

- Its proper place in your Maz. Taking a shortcut to chase self-esteem is a risk.

- The workplace is where you can really develop self-esteem. You get paid for it.

Can you recognize self-esteem in others? Keep it to yourself. You can contribute and help yourself **a lot** by helping others and recognizing their skills. Even if you are working in a big, smelly, hairy garage, you can look at some engine that someone fixes or some problem they solve and go, "Wow, I never would have thought of that—are you the engine whisperer?"

On the other side of the ledger, don't joke about a person's sensitive areas. If you are going to tease someone, which is a skill, you want to stay in areas where they are confident. Want an example—bug the great piano player about being a great piano player, the avid runner about being able to run miles, the cross-fit person about being so fit, the great person about their great hair, the math whiz about their brain, the great cook about being a great chef. You get the picture. Just be sincere. Or fake it.

Self-Actualization

Self-actualization is when you reach that potential all your teachers said you had, and you reach the potential you wanted to reach. This is the living-in-the-clouds moment—the moment where everything feels perfect. This is where people sit there humming with a smile on their face, and the puppy is not pooping (poor puppy?). Can you think of anyone like that? Celebrities even. Who comes to mind? Write them down in Table 5.2. People who have it made in the shade, whose life is perfect, who are their everything, and everyone else's everything. Try five to ten people.

Table 5.2 – Self-Actualized People

Name	Name

OK, great. Just leave that list there. Come back in a year and check it out. See how those folks are doing. Are they still living in the clouds, is everything still prefect, or have they come back to Earth and the real world?[29]

Self-actualizing is reaching your dreams. The things that are really you. The things that truly make you feel great about being you. You dream of being a famous singer or athlete or actor, or curing cancer, or being as rich as Bezos. Cool. We all do it. If someone has been telling you to chase your dreams—great. But you have to get paid, and you have to support all the levels of your **Pyramid**. Consider that. Some of us believe we work to get paid, and we do the things we really enjoy outside of work. It is hard to get paid to read, or to go to church, or to go mountain biking, or to study Himalayan pastries. A precious few people get to make money doing what they dream of doing. See the list you made in Table 5.2. Most of us do our jobs, and we enjoy doing what we enjoy doing when we can do it. Occasionally life is perfect—like fishing with your family on a beautiful lake, going for a walk after you get a raise or a promotion at work, or getting married. That is being an adult.

Moments of self-actualization can be rare. Athletes win only one or two championships in their entire lives. Actors are lucky to win a single Oscar. How many hit singles do singers get? Maybe you shouldn't measure

---

29   I don't want to spoil anything, but it is called *regression to the mean*, which is not an Ari **Mean** but a Kahn mean, and it helps make things **Normal**.

yourself against Curry, Larson, or Swift. Great to have a dream. Do you think it is impossible to get there? It isn't. Can you get there in your first job? Maybe. Can you be completely happy with yourself if you are low person on the totem pole, doing the hardest, least appreciated job in the place? You can. How? Well, back to Ari, we can be **Mean**. We can act (note how close "act" is to fake) between deficient and excessive. We can find that **Moral Exemplar**, and follow their lead and become our own **M.E.** If none exists, get another job, or suck it up and be the **Moral Exemplar** for yourself.

Sound really freaky? It isn't. Can you be an **M.E.** to your younger siblings? Your parents? Younger kids at your school? Your teachers? Your customers? Your co-workers—even at your part-time job after school? Damn right you can. Just do the right thing. Somewhere between doing nothing and overdoing it. Be courageous and dependable. Be nice at a bus stop. Be nice to the lady working at the McDonald's or the dude working at the Walmart. Give them a smile and tell them to have a nice day. These small glimpses of acting **Golden** will help you recognize what it feels like at the top of your Pyramid.

Applying Your Pennies to Your Maz

The **Pyramid** you just built is your **Maz**. You can adjust it and use it as your guide to handle your money and many, many decisions you make in your life. Your **Pyramid** identified the first place that money goes: shelter, heat, and food. You have to take care of that platform at all times if you are going to avoid harm, hunger, and homelessness. Initially, you might not have much left over after that. That is okay, it is temporary.

Routine – Experienced people use routines at work and in their lives because it is more efficient. Having a routine can save you money and save you time. Once you learn to live where you live, and you get the furniture and other things you need, then you can consider what you need for safety. Maybe you move somewhere safer. Maybe have roommates[30] to help pay for a nicer place in a safer part of town. The goal is avoiding harm, hunger, and homelessness.

---

30   Roommate Pie: the ultimate spicy buffet.

After you are settled, you can start spending a bit on love and belonging. But who do you want to love and belong to? Does it take a lot of false advertising to find them? Or should you be an **M.E.** and let them find you. That will not be very expensive. If it is really expensive, it might be time for the check. And then check around you.

As we get settled and we start being successful at work, how much money do you need for your self-esteem? It is definitely some. Could be a fair bit. Maybe your self-esteem comes from something totally outside work. Maybe all your self-esteem comes from your passion. Cool. Enjoy. Pay the lower levels first. The cheapest place for you to get your self-esteem is from work. They will pay you to do great work, which you will feel great about.

The *kumbaya* sitting on top of the mountain? Well, it will likely come a little later. It may be when your first child arrives, and you have done everything in the right order. Maybe you remembered to tuck some money away. Maybe you are smart enough to use your smarts for your self-esteem and your self-actualization. Use your money where it needs to be used. Use you to feel good about you.

Dreaming and Doing

Dreaming is a good thing. You have to have some doing that goes along with the dreaming. If you are following a dream, find out if the dream satisfies your foundation and most of the **Pyramid**. There are many lost souls wandering around our country right now because they didn't get the memo that we all have to work and contribute and pay our **Maz**. Some days what we do at work might seem a little beneath us because we are so smart, but that is okay. It is work and it won't be that way forever.

Back to the whole dreaming thing. Have a look at the diagram in Figure 5.2 and note three things:

1. It probably serves us to do a bit more doing and a little less dreaming. We have to be doing something.

2. The dreaming and the doing have to cross over. They have to intersect. You have to do something to get your dream going. You have to get something done. Getting a job is a great way to start.

3. You can dream as big as you want. Try to make your doing almost as big. Just 'cuz.

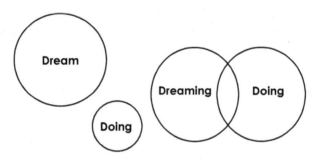

Figure 5.2 – When Dreaming and Doing Collide

Remember, this book is about your career, not your *America's Got Talent* dream. That is a different book, different author, probably taller than this author. This is a get-a-decent-job-and-live-a-decent-life dream. This is an avoid-risk dream. This is a **Golden Meanie**. It is a little on the safe side. So that you can contribute to society, contribute to your family, and feel good about it during the journey. So that you can reduce the risk of hunger, harm, and homelessness. So, you need to get stuff done.

Getting Stuff Done

Getting stuff done is always difficult, no matter where you are on your *Pyramid*. It is especially hard if you are not in the habit of getting things done yet. The question is how do you get in the habit of getting things done? How do you get things started? Well, I would suggest either an hourglass, a timer, or an alarm clock. You could use a sundial, but that is a little bit not good enough. You could buy an atomic clock. That would be over the top. An app on your phone could work.

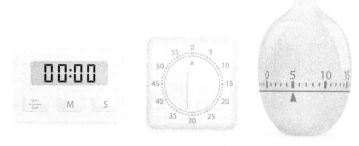

Figure 5.3 – Timers

A simple timer is a great way to start creating good habits and getting stuff done that we need to get done (see Figure 5.3). We are not really good at estimating how long things take. We underestimate some and way overestimate others. We spend too much time worrying how long things will take and how hard they are going to be. We obsess over some little, tiny detail that doesn't matter anyway. So we don't start. Our thinking is we haven't failed if we haven't started.

Try this. Get a timer and set it to three minutes. Clean your room. Set the timer to five minutes and put the dishes in the dishwasher. Just focus for those five minutes. Don't check your phone or reply to emails or texts or Snapchat. For five minutes. How far did you get? BOOM! When you get tired of reading this book, try five minutes on the timer. If this is the most painful book in the world you have ever read, and you are reading for punishment because you were late getting in last Tuesday night (what were you doing out on a Tuesday?), then set the timer for ten minutes and read. Just ten minutes. Take a break and repeat.

Don't just think about it, do it. Great piece of advice. Something to remember when you think, "I need to start my term paper." Set your timer to five minutes and figure out what you have to do. If that works, set it to ten minutes and do just a little bit more. Then leave it and come back to it in a while. Use your timer to get some exercise. Just three minutes. Repeat. Eventually bump it up to five minutes. Repeat. Use your timer. Maybe you can set a goal to use your timer six times a day to get things done. Organizing your room, doing homework, looking for a job, exercising. As you get better, you can maybe bump the time up to fifteen minutes at a time, or you can use the timer on your phone to go for a thirty-minute walk or a jog.

So how did you do? Did you make progress? If you can start overlapping your doing circle with your dreaming circle, you might just be on your way. Learning to use a timer to get things done may be a game changer for you. Table 5.3 has a list of things you probably should be doing regularly. Put three, five, or ten minutes in the empty space beside the activity. Add your own damn activities.

Table 5.3 – Getting Things Done List

Activity	Time	Activity	Time
Clean room		Organize workspace	
Clean kitchen		Make a to-do list for next shift	
Organize clothes, shoes, backpack for tomorrow		Clean your tools	
Make your lunch		Check the oil in your car	

Add up all the time, and it probably isn't a lot. If a task is a big one, like you haven't cleaned your room since you were a size 6x, then break up the task into manageable tasks, and just go at one of the smaller tasks for three or five minutes (like sort your sock drawer). Repeat with another smaller task. These short tasks, with the help of a timer, will turn into habits and become part of your character. Boom! You are your own *M.E.*

The timer is going to be a huge help when you have to write a resume, collect all your personal information, search for a job (ten-minute blocks of time, repeat). Now you have the skills you need to build your *Pyramid* and manage your *Maz*.

Summarizing Your Maz

Abraham Maslow made a huge contribution to our world by outlining some basic levels, or platforms, in our lives.[31] You can use the idea of the Hierarchy of Needs to organize your life and prioritize what you do with your time, your effort, and your money. You build your **Pyramid** based on Ari's foundation of acting **Mean** and learning to be **Golden**.

> *Consider your Pyramid as the house you're going to build;*
> *consider your Maz as the home you're going to live in.*

---

31 There are people who are critical of Dr. Maslow's Hierarchy of Needs—there are always people who criticize.

You start out building your *Pyramid* by making your life safe and secure. You need to get a job to pay for your food and shelter. You can then move on to consider the safety and security of where and how you live. Once those two basic levels are mostly addressed, you can start to consider how you belong. Remember, the workplace wants to accept you and respect you. If you are *Golden* in your personal life and your work life, you might find that you are just fine in your self-esteem and you don't need to spend all your money trying to be cool, beautiful, and awesome. Once you are on that track, you can enjoy the self-actualization when it comes along.

As you build your Pyramid, you can still pursue all of your dreams, but understand that your *Maz* means you start to intersect your dreaming and your doing. A great way to get started is to get in the routine of getting stuff done. A very effective way of getting stuff done is to use a timer to focus on getting little stuff done that needs to get done. Then you can start to tackle larger tasks using a timer to block out all the distractions that stop you from taking care of your *Maz*.

Now that you have that all figured out, you must be a little hungry. Let's learn to slice up your *Pies*.

CHAPTER 6

Your Pie

Now that we have our *Mean* foundation and our blueprint for our *Pyramid* drawn up, let's look at some of the things that will go into our *Pie*.

Before we enter the workforce, we want to bake up a reliable dish of human personality. Not necessarily a sweet dessert-type dish. More of a stick-to-your-ribs, reliable kind of dish. It would be best if we could mix just the right amount of human ingredients to offer everyone a succulent and sustainable feast of your *Golden* magnificence. It would be best if we could recognize and understand the ingredients everyone has in their own daily pie, so they don't give us indigestion.

The pie we eat goes back to ancient Greek times when they figured out how to add flour and water to make a pastry shell and then add meat and vegetables and some spices like paprika and cinnamon with the proper time and heat to meld the concoction into a full meal. All kinds of things go into pies. Some of it just doesn't seem like anything we need. Who needs to put lamprey (eel—ewww, although probably ewe goes in) in a pie? My family has a very intense chocolate pie that I can only take in the smallest morsels. Any more is too much. Such are pies. And families.

The *Pies* at work are made up of people who are made up of a wide variety of fillings. Welcome to the workplace. You only need

Question – Do you see people as made up of mostly good things or mostly bad things? This can tell you a couple things: if you find all the faults in everyone else all the time, you might not like yourself, or you are insecure, or you need to grow up and accept people for who they are. Sorry. Not sorry.

to sample parts of the different *Pies* to help you get your work done. While we are being *Golden,* and we understand we are building our *Pyramid* and recognizing people are building their own *Pyramid,* we also want to work on understanding the proportions of building blocks, or ingredients, that make up other people, or things—or **Pies**.

The first step is to understand that nothing is made up of just one thing. Your boss may not be all good, nor is he/she all bad. You are not all sunshine and roses. The politician you don't like is not all greedy or stupid. You don't spend all your money on lattés. You don't spend all your time on Snapchat. All of these scenarios are combinations of attributes. Some good, some bad. That is **Normal**.

Here are five pies we want to look at:

- Your You Pie

- Your Money Pie

- Your Time Pie

- Your Family Pie

- Your Bestie Pie

In each one, we want to identify the main ingredients and understand the measure of each ingredient. Too much sugar does not a good pie make. Too much of anything can make for a less than great **Pie. Ari**, with just the right amount of the right stuff, would have likely made a good **Pie**.

Your Pie

First, let's look at you and what your main ingredients are. In Table 6.1, I have put together a list of characteristics you may have. I have left room for you to add any that were missed. You need to pick out your best five or six characteristics, and then figure out the percentage of each of those that are in you (adding up to 100 percent). We are not worried about your lesser ingredients. Just start with the main ingredients.

Table 6.1 – Pie Fillings

Fillings	Fillings	Fillings	Fillings
Tall	Energetic	Trustworthy	Strong
Short	Pleasing	Rude	Reliable
Smart	Religious	Intelligent	Educated
Funny	Fast	Nerdy	Energetic
Kind	Insecure	Loud	
Devious	Confident	Shy	
Guarded	Dedicated	Superficial	

Let's sketch out your pie in Figure 6.1:

1. Put a checkmark or an X beside your main ingredients in Table 6.1.

2. Write those ingredients in the first column beside the numbers in Figure 6.1.

3. Mark down what percent of you each of those ingredients are, and make sure they add up to 100 percent.

4. Make a *Pie* chart inside the circle to represent your *Pie*. Divide up your *Pie* to make the biggest pieces match your main ingredients, and smaller pieces your smaller ingredients.

Who Are You

	Description	Percent
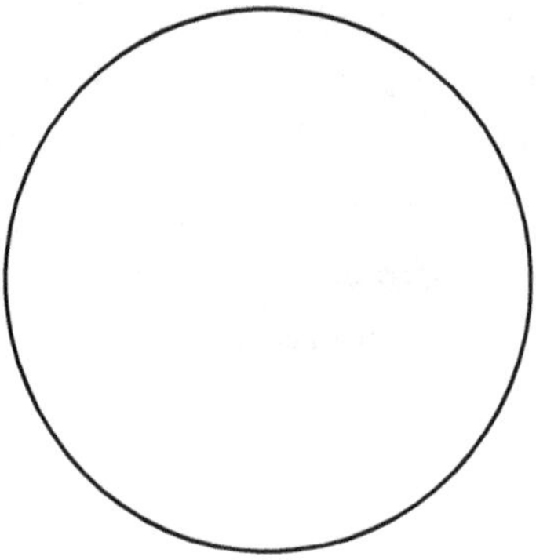	_____	____%
	_____	____%
	_____	____%
	_____	____%
	_____	____%
	_____	____%
	Total	____%

Figure 6.1 – Your Pie Chart

You can put in more ingredients if you really need to. Is it kind of hard to put in just five ingredients that make up the whole of you? Maybe. The takeaway should be that everyone, especially the ones in the workplace we are most concerned with, is made up of several different ingredients. Their personalities are shaped by their history and their *Max*. Consider that. Do you have the right ingredients for the workforce?

Your Money Pie

We should also take some time to look at where we spend our money. Table 6.2 has a list of where we might want to spend our money. You can look at this today and figure where you are going to spend one hundred dollars. Or you can look down the road a year or two, when you are living on your own, and anticipate where would you spend a thousand dollars. Your choice. Table 6.2 has many different options for you and the usual blank spaces for you to add your own options. The same as above, pick the top five or six things, and make them add up to between 90 and 100 percent. You can sketch these out in Figure 6.2. You may want to add up only to 90 percent because you should always be prepared for unplanned events. Being able to plan for unplanned events will help you avoid harm, hunger, and homelessness.

Table 6.2 – Penny Pie Fillings

Fillings	Fillings	Fillings	Fillings
Food	Bike repair	Pet food	Church
Restaurants	Car insurance	Gym membership	Donations
Clothes	Education	Car repairs and maintenance	Utilities (electricity, heat, water)
Snacks	Cellphone	Entertainment	Transportation
Rent	Internet/cable	Savings	Miscellaneous
Car payments	Furniture	Travel	
Healthcare	Pet	Gifts	

What do you spend your Money on?

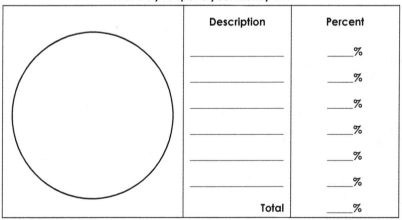

Figure 6.2 – Your Money Pie

We will look closer at the dollars you spend a little later, but now is a good time to ask yourself how much of your money you spent on your **Maz**. Did you allocate money to help you get away from harm, hunger, and homelessness? Are you taking care of the base levels of your **Pyramid**? Or are you spending it all on the top floors worrying about your self-esteem and your *kumbaya*, when a little more should be going to your foundation and support system?

Also, did most of your money go to things that are *mandatory* (like food or rent or a car payment or healthcare)? That leaves only a bit of money you get to play with. That is common. If you make three thousand dollars a month, one thousand goes to taxes and you don't even see it. About fifteen hundred dollars goes to things like rent and food and utilities—at minimum. You get maybe five hundred dollars to sort of play with. It means you have to be very smart with the bit of money that is *discretionary*. Unfortunately, you don't get to take your whole paycheck and blow it all on new haircare products or new wrenches every week. Luckily, you are smart and you are creative (even if they are not in your top five or six characteristics), so you can figure out the right amount of money to spend on the fun stuff and to get the most out of your fun-stuff dollar.

Your Time Pie

Next let's look at your day or your week. What do you do with your time? What should you do with your time? Remember that we are only building a rough guide. The top five or six things. You might want to allocate how many hours you spend on the activities below, and

An object at rest stays at rest. Start your day by doing something. The rest of your day will be more productive.

that will help you figure out which are your main activities. The list is in Table 6.3. Add what you want and then fill out the pie chart in Figure 6.3.

Table 6.3 – Your Time Pie

Fillings	Fillings	Fillings	Fillings
Sleep	Eat	Fitness	Work
Read	Cook	Team sports	
Internet	Friends	Family	
Watch TV/movies	Church	Volunteer	
Chat	Studying	Travel	
Social media	Attending school	Clean	

What do you spend your Time on?

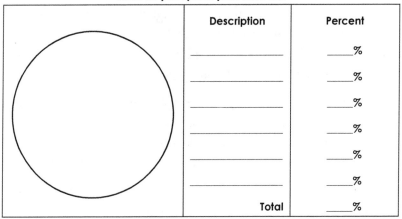

Figure 6.3 – Your Time Pie

Are you spending your time moving away from harm, hunger, and homelessness? Some of it? You don't need to focus 100 percent of your time studying or volunteering or meditating or working out. Some of your time would be a good idea, though. The same line of thinking says you should have some fun and not all of your time should be spent trying to be self-actualized and singing *Kumbaya*. It is okay to spend some time on life's more fun stuff. Relax. That is **Normal**.

Are you able to get up in the morning knowing what needs to be done, and then go out and do it? Better yet, last night, did you plan out what you were going to do today? That is a ticket to success. Do you have any parents or grandparents who seem super-organized, and they get peeved if things are not in their proper place? They have realized that things are easier if things are organized. They are simply being more efficient. You will meet those people (hopefully) in the workplace. People who take the time to organize and prepare for the next shift or the next day.

Also, did you notice that after you divvy up your day, you only have a bit of time left over for the fun stuff? What are you going to do when you are working? The great part is that work is a great part of your Pyramid, and you might feel like you are in the *Love and Belonging/Self-Esteem/ Self-Actualization* part of your Pyramid when you are at work. Awesome. Enjoy. That is a great part of work. You can feel really great at work. And you are smart and creative, and you can figure out how to decompress and feel good in the time you have available for that after work. If your job is simply to make money and avoid harm, hunger, and homelessness, you can still find enough time to pursue your passions.

Now that you have divvyed up your **Golden** personality, your **Pennies**, and how you spend your day, we can apply that to some other people in our lives. We will just do two here. Do a parent and do a friend. What are their personalities made of, and how much? Try them both out.

The Parent Pie

Your parents are from a different generation. They are obviously at a different time in their lives than you are. They have different demands on their time than you do; there are different things that are important to them. What does that look like? Without having a table of possible traits to choose from, choose five or six main traits for one of your parents and then attach a percentage to each trait. If you have a decent relationship with them, then maybe you can show them your chart in Figure 6.4 and talk to them about how you arrived at it. Consider it a workplace exercise. You are going to work with older people, having adult conversations may not be easy and may be uncomfortable, but is all part of the adulthood gig. Be nice, be honest.

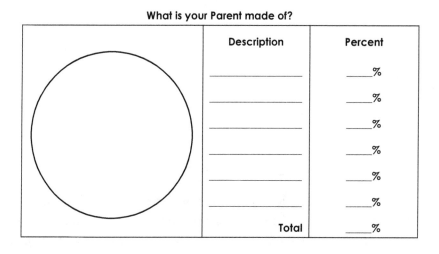

What is your Parent made of?

	Description	Percent
	_____	____%
	_____	____%
	_____	____%
	_____	____%
	_____	____%
	_____	____%
	Total	____%

Figure 6.4 – Your Parent Pie

The Bestie Pie

Your bestie should be someone you can be deadly honest with. If you are going to chart out (Figure 6.5) how you allocate your bestie's life and personality, like you did for your parents, how honest are you going to be? Are you going to use *Ari's* thinking and be *Mean* about it? Are you going to tell them exactly what you think and be 100 percent honest and possibly offend them over something that may not matter anyhow? Or will you choose the right level of honesty and strike a *Golden* chord with them?

What is Bestie made of?

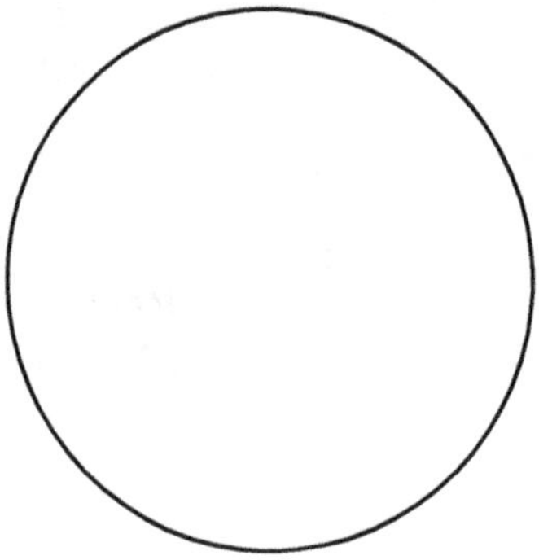

	Description	Percent
	_____	_____ %
	_____	_____ %
	_____	_____ %
	_____	_____ %
	_____	_____ %
	_____	_____ %
Total		_____ %

Figure 6.5 – Your Bestie Pie

The reason we need to look at all of this is to give you the ability to understand other people and have some compassion for what they are going through in their life. This will make you a much more valued member of any team, tribe, or workplace.

Empathy is an important skill. It is the ability to understand someone's feelings as if they were our own. If you don't have it, Google it and figure out how to get it.

It is also a good adult move if you understand your friends and family and their fillings (did you read "feelings"?). Some people may have a little too much party in them. Some might have an extra dose of anger or a smidgeon too much neediness. It is easy to see that too sweet or too salty can leave a bad taste in one's mouth. In Chapter 10, we will learn about a workplace personality named *Goldilocks*. *Goldi* is alive and well, and in almost every workplace. It will be a great idea to know *Goldi's* fillings.

Your Weird Family

Your home family and all your family relations are full of unique characters, maybe weird uncles, crazy aunts, awesome cousins, gentle grandparents. Your work family will be similar; it will have a lot of unique and colorful characters. Your family ingredients make a wonderful *Pie*—even if a little odd. Your work family will also make a unique and interesting *Pie*.

Family is a great place to practice your *Pie* making skills. Family is similar to the workplace in that everyone is different and unique, yet they are mostly the same. The bonds of your family are surprisingly strong. The bonds you form in the workplace will surprise you. Let's have a closer look at your family.

Your family will be with you when you enter the workplace. They have made you who you are. Let's talk about how talking about your family can affect your work life. We all have family. If it isn't weird, you're weird. Your parents might have had a family that consisted of your grandma and grandpa who met at school and were married and lived together for seventy years. Weird—but still *Normal*. The whole two-parent family, no strife, no divorce still seems like a nice concept. It certainly has benefits. Weird—but still *Normal*. Let's put down a few fundamental comments about families we can likely mostly agree on:

- Families should be a good thing.

- Families are not necessarily what they were fifty years ago.

- Everyone has one.

- Families can interrupt or spoil your spot on your *Pyramid*.

- Not everyone wants to talk about it.

- Not everyone cares about your family.

- Your family has taught you a lot.

- Work is about work.

- How you talk about your family in your workplace will say more about you than about your family.

The people you work with are going to judge you (quickly, efficiently, possibly not accurately) based on what you say about your family. Your family has taught you a lot. Like how to get along with weirdos (your brother, for instance), how to share scarce resources, how to fight fair, how to disagree, how not to treat each other. Your parents hopefully have shown you how to deal with authority figures (hopefully your parents *are* authority figures in your life). If you are one of the older kids, then you have dealt with annoying people—your younger siblings. If you are one of the younger ones, you know what it is like to have a bad boss (your older siblings). If you are an only child, you know how to work independently, and you know the only one who is going to help you is you. Hopefully you have learned to respect your elders, and you have learned there is more in the world than just yourself. You have to get along with people whether you want to or not. It is better for everyone if we all work together and cooperate. We always have to do more than our share. Keep your bitchin' to yourself.

If you were in foster care or are adopted, you have some special parts to your story. You don't have to rush to tell them. You are not nearly as weird as you like to think you are. Chapter 10 is specifically meant for you. Life is pretty *Normal*.

Work can be a place to start building bonds similar to your family. You don't have to get deep with people, or you might find people who are great to unload on. You might find you are a great outlet for them. They have family stress, too. Guaranteed. They just might not tell the Newbie.[32] That is okay, maybe they are just being *Mean* about it. Maybe they have learned how to be *Golden* about it—they have learned how much to share. This job is a great place to learn about sharing about yourself and your family. Be *Mean*, share some, but not everything. Share the good stuff, maybe leave any skeletons in the pantry for now.

Workmates can be a great part of your life Pie.

Through the common experience of work, you can generate some very special bonds and friendships. The bond is sometimes the work. Each task performed is a task to be noted and celebrated within the group (just a "damn we are good" often does the trick).

---

32   New staff get lots of new names. Newbie is just one of them. You may also be called Rookie, Short Guy, Tall Girl, Short Timer, Little One—all of these are in fun and are to identify you when people are learning your name. It is not meant to be offensive so don't get your shorts in a wad. How you take teasing tells a lot about you, and many times it is a form of acceptance.

Your Family Pie

Your family might have some ingredients that will give you indigestion like bad sausage on a pizza. This can make your trip up or down the **Pyramid** a bit sticky. If the family is a hot mess, it can strain your ability to get past your physiological and security needs—like if you think you are the one having to support the whole family. This could be the case. And kudos to you for trying. This could set you up for something exceptional. You might have to step back a bit and focus a bit more on your job so that you can be more helpful to your family. If the family is okay in terms of rent and heat and food and security—they are just a pain in the ass because of all their never-ending drama—then you really want to consider compartmentalizing your life a little bit so you can focus on work at work. Walk through the door at work and say, "This is now the work me. I can't worry about that gong show this weekend. Gotta worry about me. I am going to try to be **Golden**. I am going to be my **M.E.**"

Hatred says more about the hater than the hated.

97

Family should not intrude on the workplace. **Org** is paying us to get a job done. It is paying us for us, not our family. Strife in your family, like illness, will strike a chord with any other decent person in the workplace. But you have a job to do. If you have a situation in the family that causes you stress, you can use your job as your escape and you can use the stress to focus and perform better—it is better for the situation, better for your company, better for your work life. Ultimately you gain and make some positive out of the negative.

No matter what, your family is **Normal**, and as it relates to your first job, their behavior is **Normal**. Which means you may have to experience some jealousy in your family that you are contributing more than others—either because they cannot, or because they have

> There is a multitude of examples where people perform at very high levels while their life is in huge turmoil—think of the athlete who plays through the playoffs with a wife battling cancer. Think of an athlete or performer who totally tanks because their head is all worried about their DUI or their assault conviction.

made choices that became their own roadblocks to moving up their **Pyramid**. You might end up thinking, *WTF, this ain't easy, why are you bagging on me about this*. It isn't you. The doubters and the detractors will be there in every part of your life—family, friends, and co-workers. We will learn how to overcome and deal with them like the little farts they are.[33]

Your Tribe

Let's do a quick breakdown of your friends—we could call it a Tribe **Pie**. Just enter the five or six peeps that make up your group and the common things your tribe likes (music, sports, church, Pokémon, hanging out, chasing girls/guys, food). There is nothing wrong

> A tribe is a social group that has common social, economic, religious, or other bonds. There is typically a leader.

with your people. You can list your tribe members and the traits of your tribe for posterity in Table 6.4. Come back and look at it in ten years.

---

33 The little farts rarely leave a stain that anyone can see, although they take on momentary importance. But the wind generally blows them away, and they are quickly forgotten.

Table 6.4 – Your Tribe

Tribe Name:	
Members:	Traits:

You might want to also check whether those traits are likely gonna help 'ya or are gonna hinder 'ya. Life sort of moves like a river, charting its own course. The reason I bring this up is that you might want to think before you do anything that will leave a mark that lasts longer than the tribe you are in now—socially, legally, or physically. It may very well work against the work tribe you want to get into. I don't care what you do with your skin, but I see lots of young people who got a tattoo when they were young, and I am aware of two observations: First, they spend a lot of time trying to cover them up, and second, occasionally they are passed over for assignments that could further their career or give them a bigger piece of *Pie*. Your tribe is five to ten people. There are one hundred million people in the workplace. Your tribe is not everyone in the world. Just because they are doing it . . .

By the same token, your tribe may have some really strong feelings. They may have some parts of their *Pie* that are fairly extreme—beyond what *Ari* would think is *Golden*. Remember that the Internet is forever. Your employers will check you out on the *social meds*. You will be judged. Quickly, efficiently (not necessarily accurately), and possibly unfairly, or possibly what ends up on social media will not represent who you really are. Caution.

Friends are fantastic. They are a choice. They get you. They understand you. They have the same problems and similar dreams. You get to choose who you want to be your friend, and it is usually based on some very common platforms—school, sports, music, church, family, and, ultimately, work. Friends have common ideas, experiences, and likes. Your best friend can be everything to you, usually until you get into relationships, and then your partner will likely become your best friend. Your numero uno. Your bestie is still your bestie, but there is a new category in your life. Friends can play a huge role in getting started. As long as they are helping, not hindering. Some may have trouble letting go of you, and turn all nasty on you, because they are no longer numero uno in your tribe. Some are jealous and scared of their own **Pyramid**, don't know how to be **Mean**, and become critical poppy slayers. Sometimes they are easier to talk to than your family. Sometimes it is easier to talk to someone in your family. It can work either way. You certainly do not need a thousand friends. But having a few, or a small group, is a great resource, like having a really solid platform for your **Pyramid**.

Caution.

Tall poppy syndrome: This is a real thing where people try to cut down, discredit, insult, smear, or just generally hack on talented people—just because the people are talented. WTF? It goes back to Ari's time or even further. He even wrote about it (although he spoke of corn instead of poppies):

"The story is that Periander made no reply to the herald sent to ask his advice, but levelled the corn-field by plucking off the ears that stood out above the rest; and consequently, although the herald did not know the reason for what was going on, when he carried back news of what had occurred, Thrasybulus understood that he was to destroy the outstanding citizens."

—Aristotle, Politics, Book 3, 1284a

You do your best, you succeed, and still there are people who will try to take a dump in your lunchbox. Sorry. It's them, not you. It might even be your boss. Suck it up and move on. Try to smile. It just means you're good.

Your Tribe and Work

There is only so much room for friends in your work life. They may be great. They may be all of you. But they may be of no interest or help to you at work. Away from work—have at it. Hang with them, be with them, grow with them. They may help you with your identity, but they are not going to be your workplace's identity. They are not going to help you help others at your workplace. Your workplace peeps have enough things on their mind. They do not need to worry about your tribe. You have your own unique identity. Maybe it's your school. Maybe it's your song, your school team, your band, your music, your hair. All or some. Think about it and identify what makes your tribe unique. It may be hard to believe, but in ten years, 80 to 90 percent of that tribe will have moved on. And in twenty years, you might still have some contact through social media, but your day-to-day life will involve your day-to-day life—kids, family, work. Maybe still dating. But it likely won't be the people you just described in Table 6.4.

You have been told that no one should judge you, and you should be who you are and look how you want. Sure. Do it. Doesn't mean anyone has to hire you or pay you what you are really worth. If you want to stand out, way out—cool. You just may find yourself standing on the outside looking in. If you look interesting, I will enjoy passing you by on the street. I won't think any less of you, I just won't hire you or pay you anything. Sorry, that is a bit of reality for you.

I am not trying to be rude. I am speaking to you in your best interest. My motives are not that I do not like you. My motives are that I want to see people do better in the workplace. My motives are that I want to see workplaces do better with their people. Should people be more tolerant? Sure. But not on my dime. Let the other guy be more tolerant. **Org** has to survive and make money and hire more people. **Org** wants to make the world a better place to work and to play and to help more people to survive, to succeed, and to prosper. You can be as distinct as you want. But be **Mean**, be **Normal.**

This doesn't mean you cannot be unique. Go ahead, your uniqueness is awesome. Fill your boots. But in the workplace, we need presentable, normal, and helpful. Scaring or turning people off is not helpful. We are shooting for trustworthy and credible.

Your high school friends may not last through college. Your college friends may not last through your first couple of years at work. Likely you start to hang out with work people. And in twenty years, your life is your family, your family friends, and your work. If you keep friends outside of that, it is because you have a special bond—that one special friend; you have common interests. I still play ice hockey with a group of fifty-year-old guys. We have had similar experiences growing up—we got old as athletes. Your family friends are those people you might meet as you have kids getting into school and little league. You are parenting your kids together.

Your Work Pie

People at work spend a lot of time together. They like to develop some level of relationship outside the workplace. This is a great opportunity. You are looking at belonging on your *Maz*. Once people decide someone belongs, they are a bit more protective of them. They are more forgiving. Just think of your friends. Who will you forgive for dropping a latté on your shoes—your best friend or some stranger with wild hair and harsh eyes? You are likely going to get a whole new batch of people in the workplace who will have your back. It's a great feeling.

As you enter the workplace, you really need to understand that there are several parts to any problem or situation. Every problem has its own *Pie*, and no one agrees on all the stuffing. You likely can't just flip a switch and make the problem go away. Other people have a different *Pie* than you. What resources they have can be vastly different than the resources you have. When you look at your family or friends, they have different *Pies*. They are walking around with little pie charts flowing above their heads.

There are so many different flavors to fill the *Pie*. I hope you realize that. Not everyone is filled with the same filling as you. And the crust can be different. It seems like some people are all crust—like maybe a gymnastics coach or a sixty-year-old baggage attendant. It can take a lot of words to describe the fillings in a person. Learning to informally catalog your work people and to have some empathy for their existence will give you a serious leg up to help you climb your *Pyramid*. It matters.

Summary

You know what you are made of, and it is mostly great stuff. You can see the different ingredients in others. Look at the ingredients in other people. You judge them quickly, efficiently, but not necessarily accurately. You can generally see the main ingredients in others that matter to you, and you already know what you need to be *Golden* in the workplace. We have rounded out the personality traits to put you on the path to being an *M.E.* in the workplace as you start your career.

You also can divvy up your money and figure out where it needs to go. If you apply your **Pennies** to your **Maz** and spend the money on the right levels of your **Pyramid**, you will have a great cushion from harm, hunger, and homelessness.

You can also divvy up your day and see if you are allocating your time properly. You don't have to account for everything you do. Just understand that your time should be in synch with your **Pyramid**. You need to make sure that you have the lower levels covered so you can enjoy the upper levels. It doesn't have to be perfect; you just have to remember what you're trying to accomplish.

Part of adulthood is being able to measure the parts, or ingredients, of groups of people—like your family, your tribe, your workplace. Measuring and understanding these groups will help you operate in these group settings. Your skill in these areas will allow you to move from being **Mean** to **Golden**, and potentially becoming the **M.E.** you want to be.

You may as well enjoy work. You spend the majority of your waking hours working. With the skills you have, people are going to really appreciate you and respect you. You will have the whole belonging thing in your pocket. Well done. Time to get with **Normal**.

CHAPTER 7
Getting to Normal

Sometimes life seems like a roll of the dice. That is *Normal*.

You have come this far, and now you have *Ari* in your back pocket helping you be *Mean*, you have your *Pyramid* under construction, and your *Maz* helping you keep upright, making solid decisions as you go. Your general intelligence will help you put together *Pies* that apply to friends and co-workers and *Pies* that divvy up your *Pennies* and optimize your time. This will make life *Normal*. Most of the time.

Let's start at our fundamental self and agree on a few things:

- Life is a series of events.

- Things happen.

- Some are good, some are not so good. Some totally suck, some rock.

- Sometimes you get lucky, sometimes the lucky is bad lucky.

The question is, "Can you control the outcome of some of these events?" If the events seem a little random, how can you control your luck? Since life has an element of luck, let's look at it through a roll of the dice. Then let's see if we can have some control over the outcome of a roll of the dice.[34] Let's see if you can use your *M.E.* to improve the odds of a good outcome.

---

34 What happens if we try to shift the outcome, like taking out the 1 and the 2 on one of the dice—we increase the chances of a better outcome. What if we take some things out of our lives that increase the chances of harm, hunger, and homelessness?

Normal Math

If we start with one dice (or die, actually), we have six possible outcomes: 1, 2, 3, 4, 5, 6. If we have two dice, we can have thirty-six possible outcomes, and the totals of the two dice can range from two (1+1) to twelve (6+6). The number of possible outcomes goes up as we add more dice. Just like in our lives, as the number of factors, or options, increase, the more things can happen. Table 7.1 shows how the total number of outcomes increases if we roll more dice at the same time.

Table 7.1 – Dice and the Combination of Their Sums

Number of Dice	Range of Totals	Total Number of Possible Combinations	Average Total
1	1 – 6	6	3.5
2	2 – 12	6 × 6 = 36	7
3	3 – 18	6 × 6 × 6 = 216	10.5
4	4 – 24	6 × 6 × 6 × 6 = 1,296	14
5	5 – 30	6 × 6 × 6 × 6 × 6 = 7,776	17.5
6	6 – 36	6 × 6 × 6 × 6 × 6 × 6 = 46,656	21

If we roll six dice once, what are the chances that we get six 6s and the sum of all the dice adds up to 36? There is only one combination of dice that adds up to 36, and that is 6 + 6 + 6 + 6 + 6 + 6 = 36. That is only one combination out of a whole bunch of possibilities. It takes some multiplying to figure out how many different possibilities there are. For each die, there is one outcome that has the number 6, out of six possible outcomes (1 or 2 or 3 or 4 or 5 or 6 = six outcomes for the one event). If we have six dice, they each have six possible outcomes, so we multiply each dice's outcomes by each other dice's outcomes and it looks like:

$$(1 \times 6) \times (1 \times 6) \times (1 \times 6) \times (1 \times 6) \times (1 \times 6) \times (1 \times 6) = 46,656$$
possible outcomes

There are 46,656 possible outcomes of rolling six dice. The range of outcomes is from 6 (rolling six 1s) to 36 (rolling six 6s). There are 30 discrete outcomes, ranging from 6 to 36. There are many ways to roll the average of six dice; the average total is 21.

Rolling the perfect six 6s is one of 46,656 outcomes.
$$1 \div 46{,}656 = 0.00002143$$

Or, 0.002143 percent of the time, you will roll six 6s.

For our purposes, just because you roll six dice 46,656 times does not mean you will roll one set of six 6s. But it does mean it is unlikely you are going to roll six 6s every time you roll the dice.

The average roll of six dice is 21. (Each dice has an average of 3.5—which we cannot roll exactly, but it is useful in figuring out the bigger picture.)

Average of one die:	$1 + 2 + 3 + 4 + 5 + 6 = 21$
	$21 \div 6 = 3.5$
Average for six dice	$3.5 + 3.5 + 3.5 + 3.5 + 3.5 + 3.5 = 21$

If we look at the average for six dice (21), we can also figure out what percent of the time we can expect to roll 21.

There are lots of ways to roll 21:

$1 + 1 + 1 + 6 + 6 + 6 = 21$	$1 + 2 + 3 + 3 + 6 + 6 = 21$
$1 + 1 + 2 + 5 + 6 + 6 = 21$	$1 + 4 + 4 + 4 + 4 + 4 = 21$
$1 + 2 + 2 + 5 + 5 + 6 = 21$	$3 + 3 + 3 + 4 + 4 + 4 = 21$
$2 + 2 + 2 + 5 + 5 + 5 = 21$	$1 + 2 + 3 + 4 + 5 + 6 = 21$

Etcetera. Etcetera.

Excuse me while I go on to something more useful with my time than this endless game of 21. We can use some math to figure the rest out for our purposes. The math is more complicated than we need to worry about here, but you can look it up if you don't believe me. Out of the 46,656 different combinations we can roll, there are 4,332 combinations that will add up to 21.

$$4,332 \div 46,656 = 0.093$$

Or, 9.3 percent of the time, you will roll a total of 21, and you will be average. Just like if I roll the dice a whole bunch of times, I will end up average. One of us might get on a lucky streak for a while, but overall, we will mostly be average.

There are a lot more times that things will be average (in this case, we are 2,169 times more likely to be average [21] than to be either perfectly good [six 6s] or to be perfectly lousy [six 1s]).

We can establish a range from perfectly bad (6), through average (21), to perfectly perfect (36). If that is the case, then there are 21,162 different combinations that are above average, and 21,162 combinations that are below average.

21,162 below average + 4,332 average + 21,162 above average = 46,656 possible outcomes

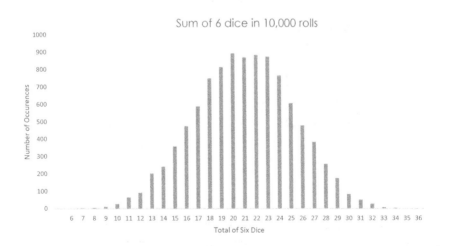

Figure 7.1 – Total of Six Dice

I can set up a series of random number generators (=RANDBETWEEN [1,6]) in an Excel spreadsheet and have them behave like dice. I can put six in a row and then add up the total. I can then copy that down for ten thousand lines. I can make a chart out of how many times each six-dice total occurred. Figure 7.1 shows the result.

In my ten thousand tries, I got 938 twenty-ones. I did not get a single total of 6 or 36. I was average a lot, and never perfect or perfectly lousy. I was quite close to average more than I was far away from average, and if we draw a curve across the tops of all the bars in the bar graph, we get a smooth curvy shape. The shape and the way the dice totals appear are said to be *normally distributed* (see Figure 7.2). The more times I try, the more likely the dice are going to be closer to average, on average.

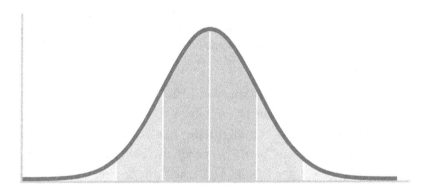

Figure 7.2 – The Normal Curve

Normal Distribution

The *normal distribution*, as it is called, represents the chance of a random event occurring. You can determine the likelihood of a certain event occurring (expressed as a percent). It just takes a bit of math, and a bit more than we are going to delve into here.

This normal distribution is generally traced back to a French mathematician in the 1700s named Abraham de Moivre. De Moivre had to flee

France (because of religious persecution) and he settled in London. He made money by being a math tutor. He mostly met with his students in coffeehouses in London in the early 1700s. Many of his students were rich people who wanted to learn about gambling and how to understand the probabilities of the bets they were placing. Abe went on to write a book on normal distribution that was published in 1718. If you get a chance to read it, I would skip it. You likely have better things to do. But it is good to know such things exist.

We have been saying things are *Normal* from the beginning of the book. We mean things are mostly average (*Normal*). Things can be a little better than average; they can be a little worse than average. The further from average, the less likely something is to occur. Things that totally suck or things that are perfect are rare events. Consider that.

Coffeehouses came to London in the middle of the seventeenth century (the 1650s). They were considered a place of communication and discussion more moderate than alehouses and taverns. Sometimes they were referred to as "penny universities," as some charged a penny to enter, but the discussion was worth it.

When you get your first job, you will likely make minimum wage or slightly above. That is *Normal*. It is not likely you will make eighty dollars per hour for your first job. You might. But not likely. You may make less than minimum wage if you have a casual job like babysitting your brother or dog-sitting for your neighbor. You may do volunteer work for free. Most people will start off at minimum wage.

There are several other things in life that are *Normal*, like the distribution of height—most people are of average height, and fewer people are taller and taller. On the other side, fewer people are smaller and smaller. One thing we can note is that over time, that average has changed. Males are a little taller than average; females a little shorter than average. The average for males and females has increased in areas where nutrition has increased.[35] Nutrition shifted our *Normal*. Remember that.

---

35 It is important to note we do not need to settle for average. We can improve our average. Average height increased due to better nutrition. You can improve your average by being *Golden*, being an *M.E.*, and managing your *Maz*.

This distribution also holds for other human characteristics like weight and foot size. For our purposes, we just want to remember that for us, some things are better than average, some are worse. There are likely more things that are a bit better than average than the number of things that are frickin' fantastic.

For our purposes, here is the **Golden** definition of **Normal**:

> ***Life has a range of good and bad.***
> ***It will settle somewhere around average.***
> ***You can control how good average is.***
> ***But there will still be good and bad.***

> ***Life is Normal.***

> ***Work is Normal.***

We want to be better than average. We want to push the curve over to the right, so that if our average day now is a 6.3 out of 10, how do we make the days average out at a 7.2 out of 10? How do we push our days into the really-good-most-of-the-time section? Life will have a range and be **Normal**. First, let's consider a couple of instances where **Normal** is a bit surprising at first glance.

Happiness and Normal

There are two events in life that yield some surprising results. Lotteries and marriage. If you won a lottery, you would be set for life, as long as you didn't screw it up. Right? And you would be happy for the rest of your life, because all your problems would disappear. Right? Not right. Lottery winners who win millions of dollars do not show increased happiness after five years. Their satisfaction with life is no better than before they won the money, even though they have fewer things to worry about. If you think about their **Maz**, lottery winners certainly should not have to worry about the first couple levels of their **Pyramid** (physiological needs and safety needs). They should have ample money to pursue love and belonging, and they can buy all the self-esteem they want, or set off for the self-actualizing journey to go sit on a mountain top.

Lottery winners shouldn't have any stress about money, but they still have to co-exist with society and their family and friends. They have a new set of issues to deal with, and they seem to replace their former issues with the new issues, and on a happiness scale, life becomes *Normal* for them (but what a *Normal*!). They have shifted their average, but they still worry about their *Maz*, even if it is the higher levels of the *Maz*: belonging, self-esteem, and self-actualization. A million bucks doesn't mean the dog doesn't pee on the rug or your family doesn't drive you crazy.

Marriage also yields a surprising curve. In a study done by a German group,[36] the level of satisfaction that people have in life starts to increase a couple of years before they get married. This makes sense because of the anticipation of a great event and the enjoyment of a relationship that is obviously working and providing enough happiness to then get married. The happiness peaks during the first year of marriage and then returns to normal by the end of year two and heads even lower than the pre-marriage state of happiness by year five. Does this mean they are actually less happy and having a terrible marriage? Not necessarily. It could mean that they are learning to deal with new challenges, and they are looking at those challenges from a negative perspective. It could be they are juggling kids, work, and bills (paying off extra debt they incurred spending on love and belonging and self-esteem in the first couple of years of marriage). It could mean they are tired, and they realize they do not get to go hang with their tribe quite so much.

---

36   Andrew Clark, Ed Diener, and Yannis Georgellis of the German Socio-Economic Panel as presented in Kahneman, *Thinking, Fast and Slow*. Farrar, Straus and Giroux, New York, 2013. pp 398-399.

So they view themselves as unhappy, when actually the joy of the kids, the comfort of the love and affection for their partner, and the pooling of the resources to take care of the bills puts them in a pretty good spot on their *Pyramid* and in their *Maz*, even though they now fart in front of each other and see more butt crack than they want to. But things are still good. They are still great, actually. Not the butt crack, the marriage. It is *Normal*. It might be a great *Normal*, and we need to recognize it. The days that suck are likely rare, and people should remember that.

Improving Your Normal

If a million bucks in a lottery and a marriage to your high school hottie doesn't make you happy for life, then what the hell? Can you make this dismal outlook on life look a little less dismal? You have to shift your *Normal*. Not a lot.

Let's consider the people around us today (or if you are working on this at night, let's prepare for tomorrow). Let's go move around and pop some normal thought bubbles around people you see (but don't *Normal* and drive—too dangerous). You can *Normal* and bus—but don't stare. How about the people below. How *Normal* is their day? How would you cut up their *Pie*? Where are they on their *Pyramid*? How are they handling their *Maz*? Three people close to your age—what do you think they are thinking? Where are they on their *Pyramid*? How *Normal* is their day? Should their *Normal* provide them with a reasonable degree of happiness?

If things are going to end up *Normal* anyway, you may as well make your *Normal* as good as it can be, regardless of your absolute situation. Let's go back to your *Pie*. How did you spend your day? Is there any room for improving your *Normal*?

Consider your Time *Pie* as presented in Figure 7.4.

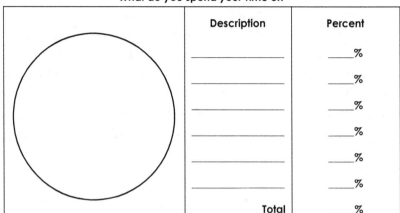

What do you spend your Time on

	Description	Percent
	_____	____%
	_____	____%
	_____	____%
	_____	____%
	_____	____%
	_____	____%
	Total	____%

Figure 7.4 – Reconsidering Your Time Pie

What did you spend your time on? Come on. Be honest (Table 7.2).

Table 7.2 – New Normal Activities

Normal		New Normal	
Activity	Time spent	Activity	Time spent

Shifting your *Normal* to a better *Normal* likely involves getting your *Mean* on and being the best *M.E.* you can be. In your personal life, it may just be grabbing your timer and adding a few minutes of things in a few different places (five minutes cleaning your room, three minutes planning tomorrow, ten minutes exercising). Remember, it all takes less time than you think.

The workplace is a huge opportunity to shift to a new *Normal*. Your new *Normal* maybe involves a little more attention to your *Maz*, a little less worrying about your self-esteem and your *kumbaya*. It means attending to your safety and security and your family. That might mean taking more time to get ready for work or taking more time helping around the home. Maybe it is getting some more education and training so you can apply for better-paying jobs, or you focus more at work and end up getting moved up the work *Pyramid* from being a laborer or a clerk to a superintendent or a shift leader or a manager. More money, used for more safety and security, more for the love and belonging in your family, and a little left over for your self-esteem.

Now is a good time to have a quick chat about college. College education is mostly great. A four-year degree is not going to guarantee you happiness, nor will it save you from harm, hunger, and homelessness. Not if you don't build a solid *Pyramid*, and not if you suck at decorating your *Maz*. It will be *Normal*. And not going to college does not guarantee you misery. In both cases, how you perform in the workplace—how *Golden* you are and how much you pay your *Maz*—says more about how you can be your *M.E.*, with or without a degree. You can be awesome at work and have a family and friends that respect all you do. It can be a great *Normal*.

If you get your *M.E.* on at work, you might find you do not need to spend as much on your self-esteem. If your *M.E.* is humming along, and you are the *Moral Exemplar*, the *M.E.*-ness may be all you need to fulfill that level of the *Pyramid*. No shiny haircare or fancy cars required. You're proud of your *M.E.*, and you have lots of room to climb higher.

Summary

Life can seem random like rolling dice. There are so many different outcomes, it seems like a bunch of dice with more than six sides each. The good thing is that you do have some control over the dice. You have control over your outcome. We simplified the outcomes into a normal distribution. That is why we can say that so much of life is *Normal*—there are good things and bad things, but mostly things will be average.

Life will not be just a black and white line on a piece of paper. Put it all together, and it will be a fabric or sheet that you can wear wherever you like. Maybe it will be a himation, which you wear to go hang out with *Ari*—even if it isn't quite as cool as the toga.

Now you're **Normal**, even if you thought you were weird. You're **Normal** and you are in control. You know you can make your **Normal** a great **Normal**. For most people, it starts in the workplace. That is what is important.

CHAPTER 8
Math of Kahn

Okay, the title is a bad pun of a movie I never saw.[37] Go ask your parents. If your dad is a Vulcan, he might get it. The **Kahn** may appreciate it. His real name is Dr. Daniel Kahneman, and he is awesome. He won a Nobel Prize.[38] I found a book, *Thinking, Fast and Slow*, written by the **Kahn**, that is about how we all think. It turns out that even though we are all different, we all think alike. Who da' thunk? It also turns out that we are all likely to make the same mistakes in our thinking. Who da' thunk? It turns out that some of it is pretty straightforward. If we know what mistakes we might make, we might make fewer mistakes. In the workplace and in life. It doesn't matter whether you are some brainiac from Harvard, or you had enough of school after your grade twelve graduation. We can all make the same mistakes.

The **Kahn** is actually a psychologist, but he morphed into economics when he started studying how we make decisions with his very good friend Amos Tversky (1937–1996). This affects our **Pennies**

---

37 Star Trek II – *Wrath of Kahn* (1982). There is also the Kahn Academy (www.kahnacademy.org), which is a free online learning platform started by Salman Kahn in 2008. He is uber-cool, too. Check it out. But this is about Dr. Daniel Kahneman.

38 The Nobel Prize is named after Alfred Nobel (1833–1896), a Swedish inventor and engineer who made a massive fortune from over three hundred inventions, including dynamite. He left most of his fortune to a fund that would award a prize every year in each of five areas: peace, chemistry, medicine, literature, and physics. In 1968, the Swedish central bank added funds for an economics prize. These prizes are awarded by a committee and are worth about $1.5 million. The prizes are often donated to humanitarian or scientific causes.

and our *Maz*. He realized that psychologists and economists were studying the same thing—people—but they saw people totally differently. We are still evolving and learning about our humanness. Hopefully we are getting better. One of the greatest qualities of Dr. Kahneman is his gift of simplicity. He takes very complex issues, like how we make complex decisions and how we think, and he distills them down to simple understandable concepts, and provides us with direction. In the

Dr. Daniel Kahneman was born in Tel Aviv, in what is now Israel. He spent his childhood years in Paris. His family was in Paris, living as Jews, when Nazi Germany occupied France during WWII. Although they survived the atrocities of the Nazis, they moved back to the Tel Aviv area after the war.

He started university and received a Bachelor of Science degree in Psychology in 1954 from the Hebrew University in Jerusalem. He went to the USA and received his PhD at the University of California at Berkeley (which is just across the Bay from San Francisco). He then studied and taught at places like Harvard, Cambridge, the University of British Columbia in Canada, and the University of Michigan.

Definitely a smarty-pants.

world of Nobel Prize-winning economists, he speaks with simple and clear language we can all understand. Subject matter aside, this is a great lesson for the workplace. Speaking and communicating simply is a gift. Too many people try to use big words (often incorrectly) to try to impress people. Use the simplest words you can to communicate your message. On to the *Kahn*!

Type 1, Type 2 Thinking

According to the *Kahn*, there are only two types of thinking. Type 1, Type 2. BOOM!! Math lesson over. I love people who keep it simple.

Type 1 is our go-to thinking. We use it the most. It's quick, efficient,

Bias is being against some person, thing, or group in a way that is generally considered not right.

but not necessarily accurate. The errors come in when we get led astray by incorrect assumptions or we pay attention more to emotions than to decisions. Type 2 thinking is more deliberate thought. It is analytical. It is tough math-type thinking, and we only use that when we have to. Type 2 thinking takes more effort, and it turns out we are mostly pretty lazy. When you use your Type 2 thinking, you can still get led astray by biases you do not know that you have. You can do the math right or wrong, or your emotions can overrule the math. Or you can do great math on the wrong issue. We can screw up either way. We make decisions based on things that come easily to mind. Type 1 thinking is impulse river (*MORE CAKE!*). Type 2 thinking is self-control, thoughtful, and analytical. (Is this second piece of cake going to keep me up tonight so I am tired tomorrow?) Type 2 can get impaired and pass out, leaving Type 1—immediate gratification—in total control. Watch out!

A great way to look at how we make decisions is to look at how we make decisions about money. How do we determine how much money to throw at each of the levels on our *Maz*? There are a bazillion decisions to make with the money we earn at our jobs. Some decisions are easy (should I spend all my money and go buy a croissant in Paris this weekend?), some are hard (how much should I spend on Poopsybear's birthday?).

Economics is what we refer to when we buy something (we are transferring wealth). There were a bunch of people (classical economists) who were considered really smart, but they based most of their thinking on the idea that all of us were all equally smart and acted the same way every time we made a decision regarding money. They thought we acted every single time to maximize our *utility*. For them, utility is the total satisfaction we get from buying something. They thought everyone acted like an "Econ"—totally rational, never making mistakes, and always maximizing wealth. Then along came the *Kahn*, his great friend Dr. Amos Tversky, and a Chicago smarty-pants named Dr. Richard Thaler.[39] They started to understand that we actually think like *humans*, we screw up, we have emotions, and we try to be smart. If we are smart, we make decisions that help us stay far away from harm, hunger, and homelessness.

---

39   Thaler is also a Nobel Prize winner in economics, and his book *Nudge* was used by the Obama White House to help set policy.

If we can learn from what the **Kahn** found out about humans and how we make decisions, we can avoid some of the mistakes we all make. What sets the **Kahn** apart from the others is he makes things simple. He can talk to us and explain things to us so we can understand. He understands that we are all lazy, so he makes it simple. Let's look how this can play out in the workplace.

Rules of Thumb[40]

The **Kahn** realized that when we have to make a decision, Type 1 wants to make the easiest decision possible. If we are happy, we might just say "Yes." If we are unhappy, we might say "No." We use our super-fast brain, working in low-energy mode, to use a mental shotgun to come up with an answer that seems reasonable and should be good enough most of the time. We use our super-efficient Type 1 thinking and leave our more analytical Type 2 thinking snoring on the couch.

This view is very different from that of classical economists, who thought all men and women always make decisions to maximize their utility. This is similar to people who think the only reason you go to school is to get high marks. The **Kahn's** friend, Dr. Richard Thaler, who seemed to like to poke a stick in the establishment's eye, dubbed the theoretical humans in economics as "Econs,"[41] and he often compared them to real-life people in the world called "Humans." Thinking everyone is going to act like perfectly rational Econs set us up for a never-ending series of failures in predicting what people are going to do. As Humans, we make a lot of mistakes when we make decisions. Quite often we think quickly, efficiently, but not necessarily accurately. Our Type 1 "decide by the seat of your pants" is often in control of important decisions that should be left to the more analytical Type 2 part of the brain. Type 2 can end up in the ditch if we let it get too tired or we feed it unhealthy things. Decisions made late at night are fraught with peril.[42]

---

40 These are also called *heuristics*—simple methods we use to find answers that are *good enough* answers to hard questions.

41 Econ is short for Dr. Thaler's term of *homo economicus*.

42 Fraught with peril is a nice way of saying, "Really bad."

The Big Purchase

So we saved our **Pennies** and we are going to get a car. That is a big decision, and it is a complex decision. You scope out the decision factors. You are definitely going to use your Type 2 analytical super-brain. Table 8.1 has a simple checklist for illustration purposes.

Lease vs. Buy

Most of your family will tell you not to lease. Go buy the car. Then you own it. What if all you can afford is a hunk of junk?

If all you can afford is a twenty-year-old car, and it is just supposed to get you to work, then consider how reliable a twenty-year-old car is. Is it going to break down and cost you money you do not have?

It is similar to renting an apartment. You are not buying anything when you rent an apartment. You are paying for the use of it. And possibly more importantly, as long as you take care of it, if anything breaks down, the owner of the apartment has to pay for the repair. Same with a car.

Leasing a car might allow you a more reliable car. People may judge you (quickly, efficiently, not necessarily accurately) differently if you have a new car.

You won't have to go through the hassle of selling the old car when you can move up. You can save up and buy a car, like you save up and buy a home.

Just a thought. Consider what works best for you. It may not be a purely economic decision. You may get more utility from your money if you lease your car and you get to work on time, reliably.

Table 8.1 – The Car Decision

Car Decision Checklist			
Type			
Coupe_____	Sedan_____	Crossover_____	SUV_____
Truck_____	Hyrbid_____	EV_____	Other_____
Year_____			
Color_____			
Mileage _____		MPG (min) _____	
Fuel Type			
Gas_____	Diesel_____	Hybrid_____	Electric_____
Options			

Purpose of the car: _____

_____

Price Range $ _____

Buy   _____   Lease   _____

Options	
4WD/AWD_____	Back-Up Cam_____
A/C_____	Lane Departure_____
Auto Parking_____	3.6L Engine_____
Wi-Fi_____	Leather Seats_____
Sync_____	Turbo_____
Sunroof_____	Tow Hitch_____
Sat Radio_____	Autonomous_____
Others: _____	_____
_____	_____

Now you have filled out the checklist in Table 8.1—you have looked at how much money you have, and what brand you think is cool. You have figured out whether you want an SUV or a crossover, whether it should be gas, EV, or hybrid, what colors are okay with you (and your BFF), and if it should be two-door or four-door. You have figured out whether you have to have a back-up camera. You call your uncle so he can make sure you are not getting screwed buying some vehicle that has been in six accidents or has been involved in a bank robbery. You pick out four possible cars that might fit and then you look closer at each car. Hmmm, which factors matter most? Which will my friends think is the coolest? Which will my parents like the best? Which will be cheapest to run? Which is the best? I really liked that blue one with the cool cupholder. I am going to buy that one with the cupholder so I don't spill my latté on the way to work.

OK, you just based your first big multi-thousand-dollar purchase on a cupholder. Well done.

Don't worry: We are emotional creatures, and emotions are a big part of every decision we make. In this case, we substituted something easier (I like the cupholder) for the complex decision of which car will be best (reliable, cheapest to operate, last the longest, give the best value). This is common in buying cars and in renting/buying homes (nice shower curtain). This is also very common in the workplace. Make the easy decision and hope for the best.

We refer to this as substitution, or availability. Our Type 2 brain got bogged down in the difficult decision of which car is better, and so we took a fast Type 1 shortcut to "I like the cupholder" and then hope it will all work out.

The Kahn in the Workplace

How does this play out in the workplace? It happens in just about every decision that gets made, even the little decisions. Workplaces get their own group Type 1 thinking going. As a group, they make the decision that is the easiest, not the best, substituting what is the easiest thing to do, but not what is the best thing to do. Groups make decisions quickly and efficiently, and often not necessarily in the best interest of the **Org**, and then just hope things work out.

Example 1: Consider 4:45 p.m. on a Friday afternoon. "Oh, crap! There is something leaking in the coffee room. What should we do?" After five minutes of trying to determine where the leak is coming from, and making sure everyone present is blameless, "I will call and leave a voicemail for maintenance." And maintenance may have left for the weekend at 4:30, and the mess sits there until Monday.

Example 2: Consider 4:45 p.m. on a Friday afternoon. "We need to get the samples shipped to the lab." "Put it outside for the courier." And the sample sits unshipped outside because the courier doesn't pick up after 4 p.m.

The examples are endless.

What was the right thing to do in each case? For the leak in the coffee room, if your boss isn't there, call and let them know. Call, email, text. When something bad happens, make sure the message gets to them. Ask how you can help. "Hey, we just noticed a leak in the coffee room. We think we stopped it. Blinger called maintenance and left a voicemail. Just wanted you to know. Let me know if there is anything you want me to do before I leave."

For the samples? Ask someone (your boss, the technical director, someone in the lab) if the samples need to be dropped off at the courier. The Type 1 group-think did what was easiest and best for the group. They wanted to go start their weekend. They did not do what was best for **Org**. Not right. Not okay.

WYSIATI

The **Kahn** has made a brilliant acronym out of **What You See Is All There Is**. It is a great tag. It means what you see is all there is. Brilliant, and our Type 1 and Type 2 thinking follow right along. Standing there on day one of your new job, what do you do? Well, *WYSIATI*, and you can't see anything, so you need to find someone to ask. People make decisions on the information that is readily available. In the workplace, people might think Billy is lazy because they never see Billy working, even though the people never see Billy because Billy is always working. What you see is all there is. That assessment about Billy being lazy was quick, efficient, but not necessarily accurate.

When people hear only one side of the story, even though they know the storyteller is biased, they tend to believe the storyteller more than they should. Have you checked the news on TV lately? This is especially true when the speaker tells their story with a lot of confidence. They may be totally talking out their butt, and totally faking it to make it, but people believe them because they sound so confident.

This is where communication in the workplace is so important. You have to let your boss (and everyone else) know what you did. Otherwise, people might choose to believe it did not get done. You have to be **Golden** about it. You can't be bragging to everyone and sending an email every time you finish the accounts payable (AP) report. But you can ask your boss if there is anything they need done because you finished the AP report and submitted it to Belinda. On the other hand, you have to let people know if something that is expected doesn't happen. If the expected production doesn't happen, if the 2 p.m. interview never showed up, if the check didn't get dropped off by the customer, no one will know if you don't tell them.

You have to use **WYSIATI** to your advantage. Don't be thinking there is some magical mystery power in the universe that lets everyone know that you are awesome and you do everything perfectly. The magical mystery bus is just not there. Just ask Scooby-Doo. The work does not speak for itself or you. Communicate. Close the loop. *Ari* would approve. If you are asked to do something, let them know it is done, and ask if that is what they wanted. Maybe you misunderstood. Be reliable and be trustworthy. Be **Golden**.

Who Does What?

Want to start a fight? Of course you don't, you Li'l Dickens. But you could. You just won't. Here is a sure-fire way of doing it.

Who does all the housework in your home (cleaning, cooking, laundry, taking out the garbage, yard work, snow shoveling, home repairs)? First, fill out Table 8.2 for yourself in the first column. Do you do any of the cleaning? Do you do any of the yard work or take out the garbage? What percent of those duties do you do? Do you take out the garbage 20 percent of the time? Do you buy 30 percent of the groceries? Now go ask the members of your household. Ask your dad (or your roommate), "Hey, what percent of the _____ do you do around the house?" And then go ask your Mom (or other roommate) how much she does. And anyone else who lives there. See what each row adds up to for each task in the far-right column. You can add your own tasks to the list, as always. It's your life.

Table 8.2 – Who Does What?

	You	Thing 1	Thing 2	Thing 3	Total
Name:					
Cleaning	%	%	%	%	%
Laundry	%	%	%	%	%
Dishes	%	%	%	%	%
Cooking	%	%	%	%	%
Garbage	%	%	%	%	%
Yard work	%	%	%	%	%
Shoveling	%	%	%	%	%
Grocery getting	%	%	%	%	%

Did any of the tasks add up to more than 100 percent? If they did, that would be as expected. Most people always think they contribute more than they do. There is a reason for all this; the **Kahn** refers to it as an *availability rule of thumb.* You can easily recall all the times you put your dishes away or shoveled the walk, but it is harder to remember if your little brother ever did. Zero percent for him, a bunch of percent for you. Same for the parents. Dad remembers all the times he cooked or made you a sandwich—40 percent for him. You made your breakfast on a Saturday—10 percent for you. Your pesky sister made dinner. Once. She thinks she does 20 percent of the cooking. That all adds up to 70 percent. Mom only does 30 percent of the cooking? Hmmm, y'all must be cooking fish, 'cuz something definitely smells around here.

Availability

Occurrence = ease of remembering

vs.

Occurrence = number of occurrences

The **Kahn** figured out that this availability rule of thumb is related to how easy it was for everyone to remember an instance when they did something (in this case, cooked) more than how often it actually occurred.

You may have seen this in your school projects when someone thinks they did 50 percent of the project when you know you did 70 percent. Or you may have very sharp disagreements with your siblings about who does more of what around the house. **WYSIATI.** We all see what we contribute much more clearly than what other people contribute. What we contribute is easy to recall and readily available in our memory. We all over-account for what we do, and we discount what other people do. This is a BIG deal in the workplace.

Let's consider the workplace. Who does what? Everyone remembers what they did, so they overestimate how much they do. They may not recall how much other people do. They discount how much you actually do. This is who cleans up in the breakroom, who enters more data, who does more repair work. It may not be spoken, but people keep the tallies in their head. Beware, be **Golden**.

Now that we know that we and everyone else behave that way, what can we do?

1. Suck it up, buttercup. Realize that it is a fact of the workplace, your family, your tribe, and any group you work with. So, do all you can plus a bit more, and realize that you will not get all the credit you deserve, but you will get more than the dufus sitting on their butt doing nothing.[43]

2. Don't sweat it. Most people see who contributes the most. People also give people they like more credit than they deserve—so be *Mean*, be *Golden*. If *WYSIATI*, then make sure people see you working and not on your phone or picking your underwear out of your butt crack.

3. Don't be afraid to acknowledge everyone else's efforts and contributions. Say "Thanks" to everyone who helped. This is you being gracious and kind. People will appreciate you more and more, and they will likely help you out as well. The workplace will learn soon enough who the snakes are (the workplace likely already knows who the snakes are). We need your help. Put a small smile on your face, be trustworthy and reliable.

Easy Answers

It always feels good to get an answer when you are doing your math homework. It is even better when the answer is right. Right? It feels great when you get a test done early. How often do you go back and check your work even if there is time available? It feels better if your answers are correct. It is so hard to go back and check your work. Why? Well, likely because Type 2 has signed off and headed to the beach. Type 1 can tug at Type 2, but Type 2 is done, and Type 1 won't win. Type 2 is too tired to give two poops about whether the answer is right or not. The questions are answered, the test is over. Where is the sunscreen?

This is no different in work. Anxiety is a normal negative emotion (see Chapter 9, *SAAGS*) in the workplace. Anxiety taxes our Type 2 brain,

---

43   It is like being in the woods with your BFF and getting chased by a bear. You just have to run faster than your BFF. Doing more will keep you from being last.

and once something is done, the anxiety is removed and the issue is done. When we are anxious to get a project done, we are taxing our Type 2 brain to get through the project accurately and thoroughly, and then our thinking goes back to Type 1, and we are going to think quickly, efficiently, just not necessarily accurately. People cut corners at the end of the day when they start to get tired and worn out (yes, work will wear you out some days). It is at that time we look for simple stories that fit the situation and give us an easy flowing river of answers.

Workplace example: It looks like we are almost out of whumpers.[44] We are on our last box. We don't have enough to get through tomorrow. We are hooped if we do not have enough whumpers.

> Wrong answer – I saw a box up front this morning—it was probably whumpers. Should be good.

> Right answer – Find your boss and say, "Hey, we are on our last box of whumpers. I think we will be out by tomorrow. Are there more on the way? Who orders them? How do I find out when they will get here? OK, thanks."

Making the effort to do the right thing at the end of a shift or a workday is one of the hardest things to learn. It is a sign of a mature, valued employee and co-worker. It is someone who will develop respect from managers and co-workers alike.

At the end of a shift, learn the difference between "Type 1 and hope," and "Type 2 and grind out the right thing to do."

Rare Events

If we understand how human nature works, and how Type 2 thinking might work when you experience rare events, you can help deal with rare events. There is no one better to explain this than the *Kahn* himself. Dr. Kahneman was in Israel several times between December 2001 and

---

44   I made it up. Who knows what a whumper is? I don't.

September 2004. During that time, there were twenty-three terrorist bombings on public buses, and 236 people were killed by those bombings. That was a bombing every six weeks. There were very graphic images of the death and destruction shown nightly on the news. The news shows death and destruction over and over. And over. Horrible. Would you have ridden a bus during that timeframe if you were in Israel?

If we take a step back—this is often a good thing to do—and institute our Type 2 analytical brain, we can look at the situation with a little more clarity. It turns out there are 1.3 million bus riders every day in Israel. Between December 2001 and September 2004, there are approximately one thousand days. That is a total of 1.3 billion riders. If you took one trip on a bus in Israel during that time, the probability of you dying was 0.0000001815. This means you had a one in 5.5 million chance of dying on a bus during that period. Less than one in a million. Would you have wanted to ride a bus? It still looks like a bad idea, even with the tiny odds. Why take the risk, any risk, when you don't have to?

As an aside, this is how terrorism works. Even though the odds are small, all the images on TV and repeated media attention cause us to over-weight the chances it will happen to us. Our emotions are triggered, and it is automatic and uncontrolled. Type 2 may know that the probability of harm is low, but the quick, efficient Type 1 cannot be turned off. Type 1 is worried. Quickly, efficiently, just not necessarily accurately.

The *Kahn* puts it this way:

> "People overestimate the probabilities of unlikely events.
>
> People over-weight unlikely events in their decision."

Dr. Kahneman calls it an *availability cascade.* Repeated exposure to the pictures and videos becomes accessible to our efficient Type 1 brain, and anything associated with the videos or pictures will trigger an emotional response that overrides the more rational Type 2 brain, which knows that the probability of another rare event is very low. Think of this when you watch the news—the media know this, terrorists know this, activists know this.

Such rare events in the workplace can be bad injuries or accidents on the way to work. Or they can be other rare events in life, like a pandemic, which is covered endlessly on the media. Now you know. Be *Mean* about such events. Keep your Type 2 awake. Be neither deficient nor excessive in your behavior.

Betting, Risks, and Dollar Decisions

The Kahn and his partner Dr. Amos Tversky really got noticed for something they called "Prospect Theory." They proved that a person looks at gains and losses differently. This was different than the classical economists always thought. For instance, the grief of losing one hundred dollars seems way worse than the benefits of gaining one hundred dollars. This difference between gains and losses changes the way we look at risk and how we behave in risky situations. This also shows up in the workplace.

Many workplaces are in business to pursue financial objectives. Many organizations exist to pursue social objectives. Either way, there are always gains and losses involved. Traditional economists used to think everything was about wealth. There are emotions involved in almost every decision, and Type 1/Type 2 thinking will affect what decisions are made ("Yay! Ten dollars more for me," said Elon Musk—not for a hundred years).

We can look at how decisions are made that lead to a gain or a loss. Again, the *Kahn* will lead us:

In Situation 1, if you choose Option A, you likely get one

Situation 1

Imagine you are given two options:

Option A: You have a 90% chance of winning one thousand dollars (meaning there is a 10 percent chance you get nothing and a 90% chance you get one thousand dollars).

Option B: You get nine hundred dollars, guaranteed.

Which would you choose? A or B?

Situation 2

Imagine you are given two options:

Option A: You have a 90 percent chance of losing one thousand dollars (meaning there is a 10 percent chance you lose nothing and a 90 percent chance you lose a thousand dollars).

Option B: You lose nine hundred dollars.

Which would you choose? A or B?

thousand dollars, but you might get nothing. If you choose Option B, you get nine hundred dollars. Guaranteed. Which did you choose? Most take Option B, the guaranteed money.

In Situation 2, if you choose Option A, you will likely lose one thousand dollars , but you might not lose anything. If you choose Option B, you lose nine hundred dollars. Guaranteed. Which did you choose? Most take Option A and take the risk that maybe you lose nothing even though they will likely lose even more than nine hundred dollars.

This is a very important example of how people make bad decisions (far worse than losing an extra hundred dollars when you have already lost nine hundred). People are more likely to make risky decisions when they feel they are going to lose anyhow. Do you know anyone who is always making risky decisions?

The risky decisions could be made when people steal, when they have Friday night hookups, or when they quit studying because they think they might not pass the test. The examples are endless.

The *Kahn* and his good friend Amos (if you have a cool name like Amos, you are just called Amos) quickly realized that people took the sure thing for the win and took the risk when they were losing. This is like a football game, in the last part of the fourth quarter when you are up five points and you can kick a field goal to go up eight points instead of trying for a first down when it is fourth down with four yards to go for a first down. The field goal is more of a sure thing.

If you are down five, and it is fourth down with four yards to go in the last part of the fourth quarter, you will probably go for it because the only way you can win is to take a risk. Football has an absolute scoring system. You are guaranteed certain points for achieving certain results. Life is a little more abstract.

Whether good things or bad things happen in life may be a little harder to determine. Are you pursuing risky outcomes because you think you are losing? Remember the Müller-Lyon Illusion in Chapter 1 (the lines with the arrows pointing inward or outward)? Are you looking at outcomes as being relative? The outcomes may be the same, but you think one is better than the other because of how you are viewing the outcome. Are you pursuing risky decisions because you think you are losing?

The **Kahn** and Amos became super famous in the university world for this type of work. They realized that losses are twice as important to people as gains are. Think about that. Losing a hundred dollars is twice as bad as gaining a hundred dollars is good. Or to put it another way, losing a hundred dollars is as bad as gaining two hundred dollars is good. This is so important for decisions we make for our **Maz**, for our friends, and for our family. If we think we are losing, we are more likely to gamble.

A gamble is something that could produce a bad outcome.

If people feel they are losing, or they can't win, they make risky decisions. Often, these risky decisions go against our goal of avoiding harm, hunger, and homelessness. If a person feels like they are cutting up a smaller pie, they feel like they are losing, and they are more likely to bet on risky decisions. Our **Maz** needs us to see our **Maz**, and override our bad decisions with sleepy Type 2 thinking to keep us where we want on our **Pyramid**. We will look at bad decisions more in Chapter 11; remember when we get there that the **Kahn** sent us. At work, you can be a huge help and a great **M.E.** if you notice when Type 1 thinking is taking over when it shouldn't, and you do the right thing instead, not the easy thing.

Summary

The **Math of Kahn** is simple. We have two ways of thinking. Type 1 thinking is super-fast, efficient, but not necessarily accurate. Type 1 just tries to come up with an answer that is good enough most of the time. Type 2 is our analytical smarty-pants side that will think things through with logic. We can make mistakes with both brains. The more we understand our limitations when we make decisions, the more likely we are to make good decisions in the workplace and in our lives.

Our reliance on these two types of thinking leads us to substitute easy decisions for complex decisions—and then just hope for good lucky instead of bad lucky. We also over-weight what is right in front of us (availability), and What You See Is All There Is (***WYSIATI***) is a great opportunity for us to show our stuff in the workplace. We can also help by understanding the real risks in rare events and understanding we over-weight the probability of a rare event. Finally, and possibly most critically, we make riskier decisions when we think are losing. We are more likely to double down when we are losing, hoping against all probability that we will catch a lucky break that likely isn't going to happen.

There is nothing complex about Dr. Kahneman's thinking. It is all straightforward. If we learn to recognize when we might be using Type 1 and Type 2 thinking, and when we might be making mistakes in our thinking, we might avoid a lot of bad events.

CHAPTER 9
SAAGS

SAAGS are bad thoughts, or negative emotions. It is guaranteed that no matter how **Golden** you are, you are going to have the **SAAGS** at work. Bad things happen. Our reactions are **Normal**. A good assay of your **Gold-dom** may be how well you handle **SAAGS-dom**. Unfortunate, unlucky, unknown events and things can lead to negative emotions, and it is **Normal** to feel each and every one of them. How you deal with the emotions is where you separate yourself from the riff-raff. It will help you step on Riff's neck and knock the Raff out of it.

The good thing about negative emotions (also known as "shitty") is there are only a few different ones. They can be identified, then measured (by you), and resolved. Even though they still suck, you can recognize them and have a plan. Remember, a plan today is better than a perfect plan tomorrow. **SAAGS** are all kinds of different emotions. They are not happy emotions. They are negative emotions. A Canadian dude, Dr. Neil Levitsky, has likened negative emotions to flavors.[45] Each of these emotions can have different flavors, but they all fall under the heading of "not great."

- Sadness

- Anger

- Anxiety

- Guilt

- Shame/Embarrassment

The first step is to understand what each of these emotions are, and then we can figure out what we do about each one of them.

---

45   He spells flavors as flavours because he is Canadian, so he must be cool.

Sadness

Sadness is commonly associated with depression, despair, and hopelessness. Sadness can occur when something unpleasant happens to us or to someone we care about. It is not uncommon to grow very attached to people in the workplace, and they move on. People retire, they get other jobs, or they might get let go. It might be the first time you realize how important your work family is and how much you care about them. It is all okay. It may be sadness about the job and where it is (or is not) taking you. You may also learn how much people care about you in the workplace if you are trying your best and have some *Golden* in you. If the source of the sadness is outside of work, like an illness or a loss of someone special, then you might choose to see work as a safe place to hang out. A place to take yourself to so you can occupy yourself and do something productive while you heal. Sadness is part of life; sadness doesn't have to last forever.

Getting stuck in sadness is what we are trying to avoid by being *Golden* and remembering that life is *Normal*. Bad things will happen, and it is normal to not feel good about them. You can get through the crappiness; you can get over most sorrow. Life will continue to happen and time will move on. When you are in the workplace, you shouldn't feel a lot of depression in the workplace. It is another great reason to be in the workplace. If you manage your *Pie* and your *Pyramid* reasonably well, there is a really good chance that work will allow you to make sadness a small (but inevitable) part of your life *Pie*.

Anger

There is no room for anger or rage in the workplace. If you are feeling that way, you got to get it fixed. Go see someone. Or look at yourself in the mirror and figure out what you have to figure out. Sure, you might get a little upset when someone does something that seems stupid, and it affects your bowl of porridge. You might feel frustration, annoyance, or irritation. Anger is our emotional reaction to something that we think is unfair.

We have to realize a few things when we feel anger:

1. People are not evil. They do not plan and devise to do evil things against other people. People often jump to the conclusion that people purposefully plan evil things in the workplace. Remember the **Kahn**, and that we are all a bit lazy. Live your life thinking the best of people. You will **Normally** be happier and no worse off.

2. We may not be seeing the situation accurately. Our Type 1 brain may have assessed the situation quickly, efficiently, but not necessarily accurately. Hard to believe, but we might be missing part of the story *Pie*, and you would be a little more forgiving if you saw the other side of the story. Maybe you need to tame your *Goldilocks* because someone didn't know how they were affecting your world by their actions. You probably won't agree with the other side, but in your *Golden*-ness you are not going to freak out and do damage.

3. We may take our anger out on the wrong thing. We may harm someone when we take out our anger. It could be someone we do not even know, who is having a hard enough time clinging to their *Pyramid*. Are you a butthead? There are acceptable ways to be angry, and there are some really bad ways to be angry. Society will not accept or put up with your anger if you are doing stupid shit. No matter what your tribe[46] thinks.

The best way we can deal with our anger is to deal with our anger. Get some exercise if you need to get it out physically. Lift a house, do wind sprints, do one hundred push-ups, or vacuum your house with really loud music so you can damage your eardrums. Make some mashed potatoes and mash the crap out of them. Table 9.1 is presented in a couple of pages. It will provide us with a process to take care of the issue. Do no harm. Harm solves nothing, and if we are going to be *Golden* and have control of our *Maz*, we have to be able to handle all of the *SAAGS* that come our way. Be a grownup. Grow up. Grow up *Golden*.

You are an adult now. People are watching, and we need your help, not your anger. Work through it for your younger siblings and all the rest of the little people that want to look up to your *M.E.*-ness. Be the example of how to deal with things when things get tough and when things don't appear fair—that will need your *Golden*-ness. Don't be a Butthead—such a *Golden* rule to live by.

---

46   Remember, your tribe is a few. The workplace is millions.

Anxiety

Anxiety is our body's reaction to stress and fear of the unknown. Remember the first day of school when we really didn't know what to expect. Or the first day on the job. Or the first performance review. Or speaking in public.

We all feel anxious starting a new job. This is what we all feel walking into a new room full of people. Totally ordinary. Starting a job? Anxious. Going back the second day? Anxious. Getting a paycheck? Excited! That is different. Being worried, scared, concerned, jumpy, tense, or in a panic is a part of life. You can try to self-medicate it away, which is stupid. Or you can grab your **Golden** undies, take a deep breath, and know the feeling won't last for long.

Most things that cause anxiety are laying the groundwork for happiness once the cause of the stress is overcome, conquered, or removed.

If you are feeling anxious—or any of its nervous-Nelly relatives—put a number to it between one and one hundred. How bad is it? What are you feeling? Fear of unknown? Are you prepared? What is your goal? Usually you can use avoiding harm, hunger, and homelessness or becoming **Golden** as your go-to goals if nothing else pops into your massive brain.

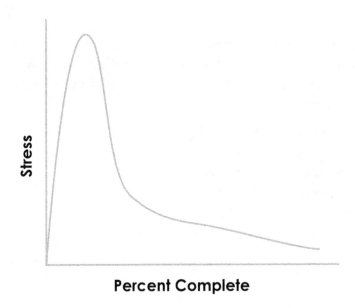

Percent Complete

Figure 9.1 – Stress Level vs. Percent Completion of a Project

The diagram in Figure 9.1 represents the typical stress curve for our anxiety. We have a lot of stress, and it will be a lot of stress until we start to deal with the stressor. Once we are dealing with the stressor, the level of anxiety we are dealing with will often decrease. Then when you are done, if you have done your best and done all you can do, the anxiety takes on an "it is what it is" feeling. Like the term paper you don't start, because you don't know how to get started, the stress just builds and builds. Your term papers will turn into not fun things, like taxes and insurance and fixing things around the house. They are all stressful with some part of the unknown in them, and we tend to put them off. Grab the timer and set it to ten minutes. Repeat. It is excruciating when you start, and then you realize you are 10 percent done, but the stress is way better. It is manageable because you are moving in the right direction. Well done. And the journey is the reward no matter what mark you end up with on the term paper. You have a plan, and the plan makes the stress better once you start.

Guilt

Guilt is guilt. You feel bad about something you have done. Whether it is a crime or an offense or any action that caused harm to someone or something. You may be the only one who knows you did it, and now you have to deal with it. Maybe you wrecked someone's car. Maybe you wrecked someone's relationship. Maybe you accidentally wrecked a hundred thousand dollars worth of

Empathy is understanding the feelings of others. If you have no remorse or just can't care what other people think, you may want to look up narcissist. You don't want to be that.

material at work. You know you are responsible and you have to live with it. There is no magic pill, no magic potion. Figure out your plan of action. Maybe it is apologizing, maybe it is just making amends. Whatever returns things to where they were before you screwed up. Maybe it is irreparable—but you have to try something. Otherwise, the guilt is going to live inside you, and it will be a long, long recovery. It will be hard to be **Golden** in that. Take it on the chin, own up to it, even if just to yourself. Be sorry and have empathy. You will feel better and feel better about yourself if you try to fix the situation. The response may not be as good as you would like, but you will feel better if you know you tried.

Shame & Embarrassment

Shame and embarrassment share a seat on the emotion roller coaster, and the concern is everyone can see y'all holding hands as you go shrieking down the abyss of "Oh I screwed up!" You may feel shame because people know you screwed up. Or you may be embarrassed because you broke a social norm. (You farted—nothing like farting in front of people you don't know.) Put a number on it—one to one hundred (not the fart, the shame and embarrassment). Being embarrassed is kind of like a fart. Momentarily, it takes on some importance, but it disappears soon enough. But don't try to fart. Or don't try to embarrass other people. Sometimes, if you try too hard, you get more than a fart. So don't try. Either way. Usually in a week or two, most people won't remember what happened to bring you that sense of shame or embarrassment. You will survive with your reputation intact.

SAAGS – Deal with Your Sheet

Now that we know the different negative emotions, here is how we are going to deal with them. There are probably a lot of fancy psychiatrists and psychologists who would do it differently. But this is our book, and we can do it the way we want. We are going to fill out a sheet and keep track of the emotion until it is resolved. You don't have to tell anyone, but you can capture that little ghoul that is hammering your soul and give it the treatment it deserves. Deal with the issue, come up with a plan, track it, and when it is over, say "Goodbye." Follow the steps to complete the form in Table 9.1. You can have a look at the form I completed as an example (Table 9.2).

1. Print out the sheet and enter your name, the date, and where the negative emotion arises from. It might be your home, at work, on the bus, at the library, or at church. Wherever the event happened that caused the negative emotion.

2. Identify which emotion it is. It could be more than one. But try to identify the main emotion, and also identify any secondary emotions.

3. Briefly describe the situation. "Bob got fired." "Screwed up presentation." "Lost BFF." "Sister has cancer." Write down enough to describe the situation so that you will understand what happened when you look back in ten years.

4. Fill out the scoresheet.

   4.1 Identify how long you think this is going to last. Did you spill something on your shirt and are very embarrassed? OK, that might last for a few hours or maybe a day? Did you screw up on a shift and break something? How long do you think that will last? Maybe a week?

   4.1 Score the emotion out of one hundred. Is this horrible, like you threw up in your boss's lap? Or is this anxiety over a performance review next week, and it is really at about a sixty? If the issue is bigger than this worksheet, then you need to reach out to someone—a human resources department at work, a mental health hotline, the police. Remember, we need your help. We certainly don't want to lose you, and we want to help you get over what you need to get over.

5. Write down a few steps you are taking. Maybe you are going to apologize for something you screwed up on. Maybe you are going to talk to someone about your sadness. Maybe you are going to gut it out until your performance review, or you are going to jog three miles a day to reduce your stress while this thing works itself out, or you are going to do a bit of yoga.

Any plan today is better than a perfect plan tomorrow.

6. Sign your plan. Legibly—you are not a celeb, you are smarter than that. Commit to it.

7. Come back and update the score for the next period. If you checked "Days," then score the emotion tomorrow, and each day until you have the emotion down to a reasonable level, or you feel the situation is resolved. If you checked "Weeks," then score the emotion next week and each week after that.

8. Update your plan if you have changed anything.

9. Sign off when you have resolved the situation. Note how long it took.

10. Remember life is *Normal*, and you can get over this.

Table 9.1 – SAAGS Deal With It Sheet

SAAGS Deal With It Sheet	
Name:_____ Date:_____ Location:_____	SAAGS (Check Which Apply) Sadness_____ Anxiety_____ Anger_____ Guilt_____ Shame/Embarrassed_____
Description	**Scoresheet**
_____ _____ _____ _____ _____ _____	Duration (check which applies) Score Hours_____ Period 1_____ Days_____ Period 2_____ Weeks_____ Period 3_____ Months_____ Period 4_____ Years_____ Period 5_____
Plan of Action	**Update/Notes**
_____ _____ _____ _____ _____	_____ _____ _____ _____ _____
Sign On:_____ Date:_____	Sign Off:_____ Date:_____

Billy's Bolt Barn – An Example

Let's consider a situation where I am working at Billy's Bolt Barn and accidentally delete the computerized inventory system, and then learn it has not backed up all the data I have entered into the system over the past two weeks. Now we don't know how many blifferdots we have at Billy's Bolt Barn, and worse, how many more we will need or whether we have ordered any. On top of that, my first performance review is in three weeks, and Mrs. Billy is personally getting involved to help me rebuild the spreadsheet. Mrs. Billy seems a bit mean. I want to puke and/or run and hide under a rock with my binky.

This sucks, but I grab the sheet, grab my timer, and set it to ten minutes. I take a deep breath and start filling out the sheet. I review the **SAAGS** list and realize "dumbass" isn't on there. I pick "anxiety" as the main emotion. I am shamed and embarrassed, but mainly I am anxious about keeping my job and getting a decent performance review. I took this job to make my resume stronger and get a good reference from Billy's. This won't go on for years, but it is not going to blow over in a couple of hours. This is going to be bad until the performance review, which is in three weeks, so I check "Weeks" as the timeframe. On a scale of zero to one hundred, this is a ninety. I feel sick about this. If I were as old as Mrs. Billy, I would likely croak on the spot. The only two things I can do to fix this are 1) to make sure I get out and walk or jog during my lunch hour to decompress, and 2) to work extra hard with Mrs. Billy to show her I know I screwed up and I have to fix it all. My *Goldenness* seems like all I've got, and it is going to be put to the test on this one. Table 9.2 shows my completed sheet.

Table 9.2 – Filled-Out SAAGS Sheet

SAAGS Deal With It Sheet	
Name: _G Ho_ Date: _4/1/22_ Location: _Billy Bolt Barn_	SAAGS (Check Which Apply) Sadness_____ Anxiety _OC_ Anger_____ Guilt_____ Shame/Embarrassed_____

Description	Scoresheet	
	Duration (check which applies)	Score
Learned I have messed up backing up computer and we lost data. Performance review in 3 weeks	Hours_____ Days_____ Weeks _X_ Months_____ Years_____	Period 1 _90_ Period 2 _70_ Period 3 _95_ Period 4_____ Period 5_____

Plan of Action	Update/Notes
Walking at lunch to decompress, working extra with Billy to rebuild spread sheet	1. _Mrs B appreciates me taking ownership_ 2. _Mr B is "COLD" this week_ 3. _Performance review went OK._
Sign On: _G Ho_ Date:_____	Sign Off: _G Ho_ Date: _5/6/22_

The next week (Period 2) comes along, I still feel like crap, and I haven't been able to completely fix the spreadsheet because there was some bizarre macro in the old one and no one seems to know how it worked, but I have most of the data re-entered. This is now a seventy out of one hundred. I don't feel sick, and the walks at lunch are helping. Mrs. Billy seems in a better mood this week.

Week 3 (Period 3). This sucks! Mrs. Billy is on a rampage. We ended up with an extra truckload of blifferdots, and some old crotchety dude (*Goldilocks* Frank) in the back says he has nowhere to store them, and they have to sit outside. If they get rained on, the boxes will get ruined, and they will have to pull overtime because they have to handle everything twice. The sales lady (*Goldilocks* Karen) says she didn't know how many blifferdots we had, so she hasn't sold any for next month. Did I mention this sucks!?! I would score this anxiety a bazillion, but apparently one hundred is max. Since I am still upright, and this can't go on much longer, and I can go get another job when they fire me, I will give this a cool ninety-five, with ninety-nine coming next week. I am already starting to look for another job.

Week 4 (Period 4). BAM! The performance review wasn't that bad. I had to sit with Mr. Billy and Mrs. Billy. I think Mr. Billy kind of felt sorry for me. They said I am doing all right, and they appreciate the extra effort. They noticed that I show up every day on time and I give a crap. They like that I try to smile at everybody, and I keep my area clean and organized. Mr. Billy said it's not the worst mistake that has ever happened and no one was hurt. He said all the *Goldilocks* in the company were just upset because their porridge wasn't just right like they like it, and they are all trying pretty hard these days because it is a tough market, and they all want to get a bonus. I am not going to get the title of "Master Spreadsheeter of the World" anytime soon. They gave me a thirty-five cent raise and asked if I needed a new chair for my cubicle.

Screw ups happen, and you can survive them. They suck, but that is *Normal*.

A Word on Social Meds

Social meds can be the source of a lot of **SAAGS**. If you find *social meds* to be the best medicine for letting out your anger and showing everyone how smart and brilliant and superior and pithy you are, remember your audience. You are feeding a bunch of swine at the troughs. They are not seeing your shining brilliance. Their Type 2 is deep in slumber, and their Type 1 is at warp speed not worrying about anything but wasting time gulping electronic slop. *Social meds* are less than a generation old. Maybe they will evolve into a useful forum, but that is likely going to take some time. TV was originally going to be for educational purposes. The original World Wide Web was conceived to be a way for scientists at different universities to share their data. Anonymous swine on Social-Media-App-of-the-Day are likely not going to step up and provide us with shining examples of *Moral Exemplar*-dom. Maybe keep your *social meds* to funny cat videos and sending pictures to Gramma. Don't let them define your life. Don't expect them to fix your life.

Summary

The **SAAGS** are going to happen; that is *Normal*, but they don't have to ruin you. Identify which one it is, score it out of one hundred, figure out how long you think it is going to last, and figure out what you can do about it. Check in each period to re-score it, revise your plan (if necessary), and assess what has happened. It ain't great, but **SAAGS** aren't great. A plan today is better than a perfect plan tomorrow.

If it seems like you have a sadness or a despondency that you cannot shake, then you have to reach out to someone to help you over the hurdle. If you feel trapped, and you cannot see your way back to the sunny side of the street, reach out. If you find yourself getting angry or pissy over things that you know you should not get angry or pissy over, or you think your feelings are causing you physical ailments (stomachaches, headaches), you might need a helping hand. No shame in that. Call an anonymous stress or depression hotline. Try your HR department out.

If it is a work incident, they may be able to help you. Your employer may have a mental health service—this is always treated by your employer as highly confidential. Or Google your issue, but just consider you get what you pay for. Going through a shitty patch in life is *Normal*. If you got this far reading this book, then you have what it takes to get through a shitty patch. We will see you on the sunny side. Good luck.

CHAPTER 10
The Org

The purpose of this chapter is to understand the work organization that is going to pay you. Your family works a certain way. It has a certain size, there are certain rules, and it has certain goals. There are certain people in charge of your family. There are certain things you can do to get rewarded or punished. It is safe to say that no two families are identical. It is safe to say that not all families are the same. If you are suddenly dropped into a new family, what do you do? Wouldn't it be nice to understand how it works? Your family is a living, breathing, growing, changing thing. So is the organization you work for, although it might grow (or shrink) slowly. The organization will be of a certain size, it will have certain rules, and it will have certain goals. Families and organizations are all different, but they are also all the same.

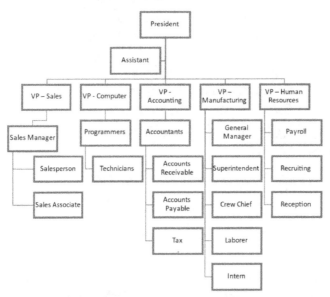

Figure 10.1 – Traditional Organization Chart

Many people think of an organization or company and think there is some sort of order and hierarchy.[47] A lot of people think in terms of something like Figure 10.1.

The organization you work for will probably have some sort of organization chart, and you can sit back in *Golden* silence as people lose their minds over where they are in the chart. This is a very simple schematic that shows some relative relationships in the organization. Unfortunately, it has some serious flaws:

1. It gives people the mistaken understanding that they only serve one person—the person above them.

2. People think where they are on the organization chart equals power. It doesn't. How *Golden* you are, your *M.E.*-ness, your *Maz*—that is what matters in the long haul.

3. The chart hampers the needs of *Goldilocks*. Everyone has a bit of *Goldilocks* in their work DNA, and the chart makes people think that they don't have to care about everyone else's DNA.

You might work in manufacturing and think the only thing you have to do is whatever your crew chief says you should do. Or you might think you just have to make the store manager happy. You need to figure out that what you do has to be reported, recorded, and distributed to all the right *Goldilocks* in the company so they can do their job.

> *Goldilocks – A Reminder: Everyone in the workplace is a bit like Goldilocks, the fairy tale character. Everyone needs everything just right. At the right time, the right way, and in the right spot.*

---

47   Hierarchy refers to status or power. The higher up in the organization chart, generally the more power or status people have. But not always.

Your Blood

Five things that blood does—all at the same time:

1. *Carries oxygen and nutrients to the lungs and the tissues.*

2. *Carries blood clotters that stop excessive blood loss should we spring a leak.*

3. *Carries cells and antibodies that keep us safe and fight bad things.*

4. *Carries waste to the kidneys and liver, which then tells the waste to either piss off or package itself for a drop.*

5. *Regulates our body temperature.*

The company you work for is pursuing a goal of surviving. The owners or the managers are trying to keep the company from closing its doors and everyone losing their jobs. The organization has a mission. The mission might be financial—"to maximize profit for shareholders." Or it may be a societal mission—"to protect all of the stray animals in the city." Good companies and their staff pursue their mission relentlessly. If they want to put a computer on every desk (Microsoft's mission about thirty-five years ago), then every decision they make is in support of that mission. If you can see how the company is trying to work together, then it is important to understand more than the organization chart on the previous page. It is also important to see your workplace as a living, breathing thing. It is alive and it is breathing. You are part of its DNA; you are in its bloodstream. Note that bloodstream flows where it needs to go. It has more than one responsibility. You and your work have more than one responsibility as well. You may work in a cubicle, a storefront, or a shop floor. Your information and your data need to flow where they need to flow (and how they need to flow and when they need to flow—and they need to get there legibly). Let's update that organization chart and look at the organization more by the groups that keep the organization moving and breathing, whether it is a four-person cupcake shop or a million-person organization. Let's redraw the functional areas and consider what they do, and how they all fit together. Let's call our new chart "*Org*" (see Figure 10.2).

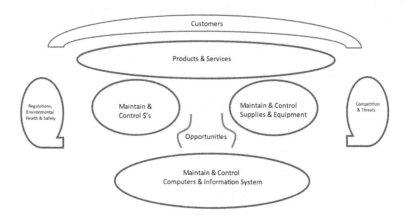

Figure 10.2 – Org

Meet *Org*. You are going to be part of *Org's* bloodstream. That living, breathing thing is going to pay your wages. It needs your help. It needs you to help all the *Goldilocks* circulating through it, even if they never get out of their chair. You may only deal directly with one or two *Goldi's* as you start, but you need to help all the other *Goldi's* as you start your journey. All those *Goldi's* are on their own journey with their own *Pyramid*, their own life *Pie*.

The brains of the operations, for better or worse, are the managers and the owners. Usually for the better, but sometimes not. It is *Normal*. At best, managers and owners make decisions with incomplete information. The managers are the ones keeping score on how the company is doing. They are trying to gather information from the different parts and to make good decisions (remember the *Math of Kahn*). They are generally balancing all the information they have with all the information they don't have. Be *Golden*, make sure they have your information—on time, accurate, legible, and wherever and however they want it.

Let's look at each of the parts of *Org* a little more closely.

Customers

Although there is nothing wrong with having no hair, **Org** needs some—usually more is better. **Org** certainly gets concerned when there are fewer customers than there used to be. Some **Orgs** can exist with just an idea (they are called *start-ups*). Some **Orgs** serve only one customer—like if you only service a single oil refinery, or you only work for one grocery store, or you only clean one house. Even then, you have a lot of people to satisfy. Even if you just have one customer. And you cannot afford to lose a customer.[48] **Org** is in trouble if it can't keep its customers straight. We love the idea of new, young, fresh people taking care of the customers. Your energy and freshness are awesome. You can start **Golden** and work your way to having a skoodle of **M.E.**-ness. Generally, young people are very respectful and polite with customers. That is very appreciated by the managers and the owners. The customers will be **Normal**. Most will be great, but a few will be from Buttlandia. One of the great things you can do if you are interacting with customers is to pass along the interesting things you hear from them.[49] Just like a beautiful head of hair—no customer loss; lots of rich, full customers with a lot of shine. That's the ticket.

Product and Services

No matter how great your customers are, you can't have any wrinkles in the products and services you sell. Wrinkles are a worrying sign on your forehead or your product line, whether your swonkydong cracks after two weeks, or your software package piles up whenever someone accidentally hits <CTRL W>. Customers have high expectations, and any wrinkles in the products you are offering will lead to fewer customers. It will definitely give **Org** a headache.

---

48   There are also internal customers in other parts of **Org**. Whether internal or external, all customers are important. We need to be able to recognize who customers are—like delivery people who pick up things from **Org**. They may not pay us directly, but they are a very important customer.

49   Chapter 13, You and Your Job

The people who work producing what the company has to offer generally feel very proud of making the stuff the company is known for. Everyone wants to be known for making great stuff, be it products or services. No one wants to have their aunt asking why their company makes crappy products. The staff who have worked at *Org* for thirty years want their kids to be proud of what their parents do. Help them out and don't disrespect the products or the *Org*. Be *Golden*.

As a new employee at *Org*, you may make mistakes. Suck it up and own up.[50] Maybe the mistake can be fixed before it gets to the customer. If your *Org* is selling a product, there is likely a quality assurance test being done before stuff is offered for sale. Samples get taken and sent to a lab or somewhere to get evaluated or tested. Generally, this is a big part of production, and data needs to go along with the sample—neatly and legibly, and the sample needs to be on time, and how it is required. The people receiving the sample will be *Goldilocks*. Don't ruin their porridge.

Dollar Signs

Some group has to keep an eye on the money. The part of *Org* that looks after all the money is obviously an important part. No money, no *Org*. Money does not grow on trees, nor does it simply appear. Every dollar is tracked. There are lots of laws the owners and managers have to watch—they can't take the money and just head to another country and live on the beach. At least not legally.

Any *Org* that has more than just a few people will have an accounting department keeping their eye on all the money. It takes people who are very dedicated and willing to track down every penny. They get *Goldilocksey* because it is their job.

There are people who work in *accounts payable (AP)*. These people have to make sure all the bills are paid, and that everything that gets paid for is actually received. Think about it: Would your parents give you a credit card and just say, "Buy what you think we need, and we will just pay the

---

bill when it arrives," no questions asked? Probably not. Your parents probably want to know what you are going to buy beforehand, and then they are going to want to see a receipt. It says, "Yes, the money got spent on what it was supposed to get spent on." The AP people have to make sure to pay the bills for utilities to keep the heat on, pay for all the raw materials so the people that sell us the raw materials will keep selling us raw materials, pay all the taxes, pay all the contractors—maybe an electrician comes in and fixes some equipment—the cleaning company, the couriers, the uniforms, the sales brochures, and so on. There has to be enough money to pay for all that.

To make sure there is enough money in the bank to pay for all that, *Org* needs to keep producing stuff to sell, and there are usually people who work in *accounts receivable (AR)*. These

There are three types of customers Org does business with:

B2C – business to customers

B2B – business to business

B2G – business to government

people make sure all the customers pay their bills so there is money to pay all of *Org's* bills. The payments have to be collected from the customers on time, or there isn't enough money for AP to pay all the bills. Think about working, not getting paid, and having to pay rent. *Org* has to pay for its rent—it needs its money.

If you work in a restaurant, customers pay you for their meal as soon as they are done eating. In fast food, they pay as soon as they order their food. That is an example of a B2C, or business-to-customer Org. Many *Orgs* deal in the B2B, business-to-business, and B2G, business-to-government, markets. Selling raw materials to a manufacturer is an example of B2B. Fixing a pothole in a road is an example of B2G.

If you are selling to a B or a G, it is generally done on credit. The customer has to have credit set up with the AR department. Then the AR has to receive all the information it needs (clearly, legibly, immediately, however they need it), so they can bill the B or the G. These customers are *Normal*. Most are great, but some will not pay their bill if there is any little thing wrong with it. If you are anywhere in the process, you have to make sure you are doing your part. If you do, you will be *Golden*—just for doing what you are supposed to be doing. There is no magic in that. Many smaller **Orgs** have great products and services, but their AP and their AR are a hot mess—the money can't get to where it needs to go. You can step in and be **Golden** if you put the energy into figuring it out.

There are more parts to the money part of **Org**, but you get the idea. Money matters. Don't waste it. Track everything you do. Keep records, keep notes, keep receipts and packing slips and invoices. Do your part so it can get to the **Goldilocks** that needs it.

Equipment & Stuff

There has to be a group that keeps an eye on all that the **Org** uses and owns. You might work for a company that owns a half-ton truck, a lawnmower, and a rake. Cool. The half-ton, the lawnmower, and the rake have to be taken care of. There has to be gas for the truck and the lawnmower. If they go down, there is no way to make money to pay for more gas to get to the next job, no way to mow the lawn once you get there, and no way to clean up after mowing the lawn. Certainly, there is no money to pay you for all your hard work. Equipment and stuff have to be taken care of. Many entry-level jobs start with taking care of the things that **Org** owns. An example is floors. Sweeping floors is done to take care of the floor and stop the floor from being an injury hazard or to stop dust from being a breathing hazard for everyone. For a new employee, the idea is that while you are sweeping the floor, you are learning everything else that is going on at **Org**. Being **Golden** means you are engaged and you care. Even if you cannot connect the dots as to why you have to sweep a floor that is just going to get messy again.

The long-term staff at **Org** care and have invested years of their lives and have built their **Pyramid** with the help of **Org**. They have developed their **Maz** thanks to **Org**. They can turn complete Shinnok[51] on you if you can't do your part. Many people have learned to be clean and organized by learning to be clean and organized in their work life. Then they learn

---

51 Mortal Kombat – Pure Evil.

it is an easier way to live, and it ends up saving time and money at home. The workplace is a great place to learn how to make your life better.

Even if you work on the dollar side of *Org*, you may need to help the people who work with the equipment and stuff. If a bill sits on your desk without getting paid because you don't understand what a schwingledoodle is, you may ruin *Goldilocks'* day, and this *Goldilocks* may be a big hairy dude who really needs your help.

> Due diligence is a term that refers to doing your part to make sure something is right— like making sure a part is received. It usually has a piece of paper for confirmation and evidence of authorization from someone higher than you in the Org.

You may shut down their production because it might be a component to one of the key pieces of machinery. Be *Golden*. Don't let stuff sit because you don't know what it is. Being *Golden* is making sure you ask questions to keep things flowing through *Org*. The same thinking says you want to make sure the schwingledoodle is needed, or make sure it is a real thing that is really needed. Someone should have authorized the purchase. The Newbie who has been working at *Org* for two weeks shouldn't have ordered ten thousand schwingledoodles without getting permission from someone and having some documentation of that permission. You need to find out how that process works, whether you need the parts to do your job, or if it is your job to order and arrange payment for the parts.

Hopefully, your *Org* has some good processes in place to make sure things are bought in a wise way. You probably don't have fifteen boxes of cereal at home. *Org* doesn't need a ten-year supply of supplies. But *Org* does need to have some supplies so that its production and operations do not come to a halt because a two dollar part is not available. Some *Orgs* are very organized. Some *Orgs* are pretty chill in this area. Some *Orgs* are a bloody mess. Your goal is to start *Mean*, figure things out, be *Golden*, and help out. There is often lots of room to be the *M.E.* Start off by trying to not be the one who brings things to a full stop because you wrecked equipment or you didn't tell anyone that you were almost out of supplies. Things do not magically appear unless you work with some dude who has a lightning bolt on his head, has a pet owl, and arrives at work on a Nimbus 2000.

Computers in the everyday workplace are two human generations old. Maybe three, tops. When computers started entering the workplace in the 1960s and 1970s, they were for large, repetitive tasks and for simplifying complex calculations (Figure 10.3). Then they helped with word processing, and we got computers on our desks with pre-programmed software packages like Excel and Word in the mid-1980s. OK, that is super simplifying it, but things have changed very fast. Your knowledge and ability as adopters and users of computers is unparalleled. Mostly it is because you are *Golden* with computers. They do not scare you. The old codgers you are going to work with may still be intimidated by computers in the workplace, even though at home they build their own automatic surveillance systems out of old video cameras and a toothbrush. They know more than you think they do, and you may not be as smart at programming things as they think you are. It all sets up for a *Goldilocks* smackdown. Good time to cool your coolness and try to be *Mean* with your computer skills before you show your *Golden* side.

Computers & Information Systems

Garbage into computers, garbage out. Nothing into a computer, nothing out. Let's begin.

Most **Orgs** now run an **Org**-wide computer system that tries to take in all the information and stuff from all the different **Org** organs (AR, AP, accounting, production, human resources, tax, regulation, paper clip inventory) and tries to make the computer spit out the meaning of life. Even if you successfully put in all the different types of data, the best you can hope for is **Org**-Christmas computer fruitcake—most of the data-fruitcake doesn't get consumed, and the data just sits there unconsumed until it goes to data heaven (or wherever unused data goes) until the party is over. But you still have to have it. Just like you have to have some of your aunt's fruitcake, and you have to like it. You have to help with the fruitcake at home and at **Org**. Note that the computer fruitcake does spit out financial information that is important for keeping track of how **Org** is doing, and for filing information with the government.

The government has some fruitcake eaters that need to be fed.

Even if the computer system seems like a pile of garbage, and it is hard to enter even the simplest data, it still has to get done. And it doesn't cut you any slack because you are new. Many workplaces use the computer as their timeclock. You have to clock in on the computer when you arrive, when you take breaks and when you leave. *Org* needs accurate information so it can pay you correctly and legally. You need to enter all your pension and healthcare choices when it tells you to enter all your choices. You will get paid to do it all. It is not like a school history paper

The IBM System/360 was *the* mainframe computer in the last part of the 1960s and 1970s (> one hundred and thirty thousand dollars). Today's smartwatch is about sixty thousand times more powerful.

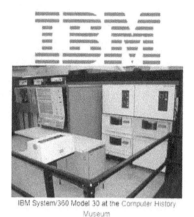

IBM System/360 Model 30 at the Computer History Museum

Figure 10.3 IBM System/360

that you can ignore because it doesn't affect your life. Be *Golden*, be the one who gets everything entered into the computer system as required. Be reliable, be trustworthy. People will notice.

Regulations

It may not seem like all the safety and environmental regulations affect you, but *Org* is monitoring all the regulations, making sure everyone is following safety rules and regulations, and making sure everyone is following all the environmental rules and regulations. There are two reasons:

1. *Org* cares about you and your safety. It does. The owners and the managers truly care on a very human level. They do not want you to get hurt. New employees are more likely to get injured on the job. Newbies haven't quite figured how to do things yet and they try, but sometimes they don't do things the best way, so they end up hurting themselves. Everyone has gone through it. Your work

family cares about you. Even if you are an ass, the workplace is a caring place.

2. *Org* cannot afford for you or anyone to break the rules and regulations. The fines and the hassles are far too expensive. Everyone at *Org* is pulling together in the very competitive world, and it cannot afford to pay the fines, which have become very expensive, and *Org* cannot afford all the time and attention (negative) that comes from violating any city, state, or federal health, safety, or environmental regulations. No one wants to go home and tell their kids they polluted the river.

Org also has to be watching out for new regulations that can hurt the company and everyone in it. It costs money to follow regulations—but not as much as not following the regulations. *Org* is trying to survive and wants to keep employing you. Help it out.

Competition

Org is trying to survive and wants to keep paying you—help it out. It is intensely competitive out there, in any market. Most markets have more things than are needed. There are likely more cupcakes supplied than can possibly ever be eaten. There are not enough car buyers to even come close to soaking up all the cars that are produced. There is more oil and gas than is needed, and stuff comes into our country from other places that do not have the same standards as we have. Other countries do not have the same health and safety regulations. Other countries burn cheaper, much dirtier coal for their power. Other countries don't pay the same wages, nor do they offer the same health benefits or have the same payroll taxes. We have to overcome all that by being better. We need your help.

There are always new products coming onto markets that disrupt the market and can put *Org* out of business. Progress happens slowly. Progress can slowly eat *Org's* lunch and leave *Org* with an empty belly and empty cupboards. Then **Org** can't pay its payroll, and things can happen very quickly.

Managers and owners are continually positioning the company to advance, progress, or evolve—just to survive. If they miss a market opportunity or a change in the market, **Org** could be DOA. It matters if you cut some slack to the managers and owners—be nice, say "Thank you," and wish them the best. They are out busting it for you.

Eastman Kodak was the name in cameras through most of the twentieth century. All of those pictures in those frames at Gramma's were likely taken on a Kodak camera and printed on Kodak paper. At one time in the twentieth century, Kodak sold 85 percent of the cameras and 90 percent of the film. Kodak invented a digital camera in 1975, but was bankrupt by 2012 mostly due to digital cameras and cameras in phones, which started appearing in the early 2000s. Kodak is now trying to make medical equipment. A lot of people lost their jobs.

Opportunities

The marketing and sales staff are in constant contact with customers. They hear the complaints. They hear about product flaws or billing issues or late shipments or shipments that are missing pieces or components. They listen to what the customers want and what else the customer is buying, and then report it back into the bloodstream at **Org**. Opportunities are what allow **Org** to grow and to evolve. It can't happen if **Org** is spewing crap out onto the market. If you have a horrible taco from the bad taco truck, do you really want to try the new vegan gyro from that taco truck? Probably not. Your **Golden**-ness and your commitment to **Org** will help it put out good products and services and allow **Org** to develop new products and services that people will want to try. You are part of that from the start. The customers and the market are the ultimate **Goldilocks**.

Summary

All of this stuff is rolling around in management's head and flowing through *Org*. It is a synchronized dance that needs to be done in harmony so that *Org* stays healthy and happy. You have a place in *Org*. You can be so helpful to a great group of people who need your help. They will appreciate and respect you even though they all have *Goldilocks* tendencies.

When things go right, a lot of companies reward their employees with a bouncy baby bonus. Maybe once a year. Your first bonus will be much smaller and much more valuable than you think. You may get a bonus because *Org* is really healthy, and everyone gets one. Or you may get a bonus because you yourself are the *M.E.* you want to be, and everyone appreciates you. Well done. That is a long way from harm, hunger, and homelessness. Well done.

CHAPTER 11

Severity

If you are in or have ever been in the foster care system;[52] if you have lived in a world that is always being disrupted by the police, absentee parents, parents with substance abuse issues, or physical abuse issues; if you have had multiple (three or more) stepparents that you have had to keep getting used to; if you have been through numerous schools or been shuffled between the homes of various relatives; if you have gone to various schools during any given school year or feared being torn from your brothers and your sisters; if you feel you have always had to be on guard, because some uncontrollable force is going to rip things away from you, this chapter is for you. You can make it.

This chapter is directed at people who have been in foster care and have been directed to read this chapter. The chapter is a good review of the information in the book.

There are valuable jobs where you can succeed.

There are people who just want to respect you for being you, not you and your baggage. They want to respect you and all your skills and your talent. They want to respect your abilities and your willingness to help. The workplace is an opportunity for you to have some control over your life. You get some control over how much money you have, and you get some control over who you let inside your life and who you work with. The workplace cannot replace some of the things you have missed out on, but the workplace can provide a lot of things so that you don't have to miss out on very great things going forward. And this is true whether

---

52   I have not been a foster child. My wife and I have been foster parents for many years. We have fostered babies, toddlers, and teenagers, all with varying degrees of success, for varying periods of time. We have seen the looks in their eyes, their broken hearts, and their fear and anger.

you have had enough of school and are ready to enter the workforce, or you just need to enter the workforce to get some cash to go back to school. The workplace is a family where you get treated like an adult and you get to be an adult.

We want you to live like an adult[53] so you can take care of your finances, your family, and your friends—for the health of it. You can live a *Normal* life with its *Normal* ups and downs. You can avoid hunger, harm, and homelessness.

We cannot solve your family problems—that will take years and years. But we can put you on a path to success. Not Ferrari, hot crib, loser gangster style. More a style that says,

"I have a job and some money saved up, I live a bit modestly and carefully in a reasonably nice area with other mostly reasonably nice people, and I am in a decent relationship."

More tranquility than trashy, more virtue than volatility, more safety than sexy, where life is *Normal* (see Chapter 7)—it has its ups and downs, but you can handle most of them without complete devastation each time something goes wrong. Without having to hit the "reset your life button" every time something happens. Without complete catastrophe. Without having to start from zero every time.

Success

You can succeed. You can lead a life that feels good, that you enjoy most of the time and can be proud of. That is the beauty of working. There is a group of people that want you, and they want your help. They want you to succeed because if you succeed, they are more likely to succeed working with you. They want you to be part of their work family. They

---

53   Having kids before finishing your education and getting married is a recipe for poverty. Adults don't bring children into this world "by accident." They don't bring children into this world with someone who is not going to stick around, help pay the bills, and take care of the kid until they grow up and become an adult. And they don't bring more children in the world than they will ever be able to afford. Kids need adults for parents.

want you to help them do their jobs, to be a part of their team, and that will help them with their life-journey. They know it is best for them if they help you and you help them. You can contribute to their day, while they help you with yours. They will not judge where you come from. (They may kid you, they may joke with you, they may have a bit of fun with you.[54]) You do not have to tell them about the monsters in your closet or the ACEs up your sleeves. You just have to start with some very simple things:

> **Appear** – Show up for work. On time, every day. You have to show your co-workers that you are not a jackass who cannot be trusted, you are not a selfish person, and that the job—yours and theirs—matters. You can't help your co-workers if you don't show up. They can't like you if you don't show up. We are shooting for trustworthy and credible, even if you have to fake it a bit.

> **Modesty** – Bury a bit of your coolness and let this job be important to you. Even if it is only a part-time job and you have every intention of moving on to something bigger and better. Even if this job is a little beneath you. Make this job important. Make it matter. Care. The job and the people at the job are ready to care about you.

> **Help** – It is okay to ask for help. You cannot possibly know everything. You are not showing weakness by asking questions. People will start to respect you more if you have the strength to show a little weakness. If you are willing to show a little humility, a little modesty, a little moderation, it goes a long way (Chapter 2).

---

54   One of the biggest signs that people are accepting you is that they tease you. They poke a little bit of fun of you. There is a difference between bullying and teasing. Teasing can be a form of social acceptance. Bullies are generally insecure assholes who try to hide their insecurity and loser-ishness by trying to make other people feel small or afraid. Teasing is poking a bit of fun over something you are good at or something that doesn't matter. You have to learn to trust in the difference between the two.

Effort – Put effort into it. Try at your job, and try to be safe, clean, and organized. Work. Be willing to learn. If you are opening envelopes, do it with a smile on your face.[55] If you are cutting hair or putting files away, show you care.

Learn – Take the opportunity to give someone the opportunity to teach you. There are people who want your help, and they get to pass on wisdom that you can use to make more money and to make more of your life.

Laugh – Be willing to laugh at yourself a bit. It is okay if you are not perfect. In fact, people will likely prefer you a bit if you are not perfect. They're not perfect either. You can check out if they are not cool enough to admit it. They may not be. People are *Normal.*[56]

These are guidelines for you to follow. You already know them. We are just reminding you so that you bring them with you. In the rest of the chapters of this book, we lay a foundation and a structure so you can go into the workplace and be successful, whether you are working as a hot-shot lawyer or you just took a job sweeping floors to pay bills for the time being.

What Is Success?

This book is not about being a gazillionaire, or a BET gangster, or a YouTube star. This is about living without ongoing fear of harm, hunger, and homelessness. We are going to consider ourselves successful if we make an average-to-above-average amount of money and live an above-average life.[57] Everything above that is a bonus. We are going to feel

---

55   We look at how to act and how people judge you in the workplace in Chapter 3.

56   Chapter 7. It is really important you understand *Normal.*

57   Chapter 3 talks about living a life in the *Golden Mean*. You might want to give it a read when you are done with this part. It talks about living a cool life so you can feel good and so others want to be like you.

good about who we are because people we interact with every day mostly respect us and mostly like us.[58] We are going to handle our money well and make fewer poor decisions than most people. We are not going to contribute to the scum that make our neighborhoods and cities scummy. We are not going to support organized crime.[59] We are going to support families, even if ours hasn't been perfect so far. We know the idea is right. We are going to have more fun than most people because we are going to earn our fun and we are going to choose how we have that fun. We are going to grow up and prepare ourselves to have a relatively normal family (if you currently have a normal family, you're weird). You will have better relationships and money in the bank. Does all that other crap matter anyhow?

You can strive for the sky, chase all your dreams, and pour your heart and soul into your passions. If you avoid harm, hunger, and homelessness, and you mostly contribute at the workplace and to your work family, you are a success. You will feel good about it. Simple recipe. Simple life. Simple success.

What Is Failure?

See if this makes sense: A person doesn't have much money, so they don't even look for work, because they can't make a million dollars and get a Ferrari, so why even try? They accept they are not going to be rich, so they choose to live in a tent and eventually start taking drugs and become more of a burden on their family and society. They live without running water or walls or heat and warmth because they are not going to be rich anyway. The downward spiral takes resources—like money and energy and love—away from their family, as the family tries to reach out and help them. They suck their kids and their parents into it, so everyone

---

58 The Tall Poppy Syndrome guarantees us that not everyone will like us. No matter what. Sometimes, the better we are, the more people seem to want to chop us down. But only a few. We chat more about this in Chapter 6.

59 The same people who are selling the drugs are running sex slavery, child slavery, kidnapping, and extortion. You protest people because you disagree with their politics, but you support these idiots?

can be helpless just like them. Or is there a better way? There is. That is what this book is about.

Or try this: You can't get a good job because you can't pass an entry-level drug test for a decent-paying job. We talk about pre-employment drug testing and random drug testing in Chapter 12. Or you have kids before you get married so you can never get your head above water and provide for your kids. Or you get saddled with child support for a kid whose life you may or may not get to be a part of.

There are lots of opportunities for failure. They are mostly avoidable. Trying and losing is not failure. Being a screw-up—that is failing. Make sure you check out Chapter 12.

Your Gifts

You have been given two gifts that you may not have wanted but can use. Life may have given you some crap that you wish you had not been given, but these two skills are extremely useful in the workplace.

> **New Situations** – You are used to new situations and the anxiety that goes with it. Going through a new door where everything is foreign and the rules are different and you do not know what the expectations are or what is expected of you is nothing new to you, just like your first day of work. While you still may view it as unpleasant or stressful, you have survived it before, and you can survive it again. This book will help you thrive if you chew through the whole thing.

> **Having Nothing** – You are used to getting by with very little—very little dollars, very little direction, and very little support. You know how to survive. It doesn't take you a gazillion dollars to avoid hunger, harm, and homelessness. It takes some work, some thought, and a plan. Initially, you may not get a lot of direction at work as to what the rules are, but you can likely figure most

of them out. You don't start out in your career making a
lot of money. You know how to focus on what matters.[60]
You are a little tougher emotionally, a little more resilient.
You can put that to some good use.

In Table 11.1, let's look at some of the other characteristics you may
have that the people who have been given everything on a silver platter
may not have.

Table 11.1 – Success Words

List some characteristics that help people succeed. What do the words mean?
Add some word of your own:

Grit - _____

Determination - _____

Resiliency - _____

Toughness - _____

Perseverance - _____

Industriousness - _____

_____ - _____

_____ - _____

_____ - _____

_____ - _____

---

60 When you meet the *Maz* in Chapter 5, you are going to learn how to put your money
where it matters most.

Sometimes we cannot see the gifts that are right in front of us. Can you think of any other things you are really good at? I know one more thing.

Procrastination

Procrastination[61] is one of the best skills you have learned so far in your life. When was the last time you cleaned your room? Or updated your budget? Why not? How about re-folding your T-shirt drawer? Organizing your pictures on your phone? Phoning your grandparents? You put off all these things. You are awesome at it.

You know you should do all those things, and it isn't the end of the world if you don't. But it is waaaayyyyy better if you do them. If you do more of the things you should do instead of wasting your time away staring at your phone, you will open up all the time you need to do all the things you know you should do.

Let's make another small change. Let's procrastinate doing some things we already know we shouldn't be doing. If you haven't started using drugs, then put if off a while longer. If you have, let's not do it again. Just not today. Repeat that same thought tomorrow. And the next day. Maybe don't have the Jack and Coke, or the six wine spritzers, or the six-pack of beer. Just not today. Maybe tomorrow. Repeat. Put off having the triple burrito deluxe or the three double cheeseburgers, the seven Diet Cokes, the massive bag of chips. Put off stealing. Put off the bad things, the wrong things. Just today. Repeat tomorrow. Get your steps in today. Go for a walk, go to the library, go to the gym. Stop by a church. Jog for three minutes. Use the stairs. Read a spiritual text. Just today. Repeat tomorrow.

Use your procrastination skills to put off the things you know are wrong. Just for today. Repeat tomorrow.

If you can avoid the bad decisions for a while, you will find yourself feeling better. It will not be immediately apparent. It takes a bit of time.

---

61   Procrastination is the art of delaying or postponing something.

Then you slowly start to go, "Wholly crap,[62] this feels pretty good. I am going to do this for one more day." I am going to put off the bad stuff one more day. What can I do with the extra time because I have more energy and I don't feel like shit? What can I do with the extra money because I didn't blow it on some stupid shit? Besides, I really don't want to support organized crime, so I am going to stay away from supporting those idiots.

How can I do more of the good things that I know I should do, but I never get around to? Well, we learned that in Chapter 5.[63] Go buy a little kitchen timer, set it to three minutes, and go clean your room. Set it to five minutes and go clean the kitchen. The little things teach us things:

1. The timer helps us focus on the task at hand and shut out all the distractions.

2. All those little things do not take very long.

3. Doing good things doesn't take very long.

Learning to get stuff done will put you miles ahead of most other people. Even the little things that you don't think matter, like being neat at work and writing a little daily to-do list at work. Getting stuff done is a great skill that will help you shine no matter what your background is, what your address is, what your income is, or what your GPA is.

Misconceptions

There are often some misconceptions that the only people who succeed are the already rich who have everything handed to them. There is this idea that some are "so smart they can't fail." The expectation is that life just rolls out in front of some people with rose petals and harp music. Not so. Life is *Normal*.

---

62   Or Holy crap. Or Holey crap. Your choice.

63   In Chapter 5, we figure out how to get things started and how to get them done.

What Success Is – We need to make sure we understand what making it is and what success looks like. Remember, this book is about avoiding harm, hunger, and homelessness. If you think it is about making it in the gangster lifestyle, please read another book. (If this is the case, you may as well borrow the book from a library, 'cuz you are likely going to get shot—no sense wasting money buying the book.)

If we define success right, then we will avoid a lot of disappointment. *Maz* up! You need to pay for the important things like food and rent before you start buying yourself trinkets to hide your poverty. A lot of people buy things in the wrong order, and they get stuck with lots of bad debt because they are trying to hide what they think of as the shortcomings in their life. They spend too much money buying designer things, expensive electronics, trendy clothes, trying to hide behind flashy trinkets.[64] News flash—no one cares. No one cares if you waste all your money on stupid things, and they don't care if you don't have all those stupid things. At the end of the day, you learn that the joy of buying a trinket doesn't last very long. Buying a trinket will not erase the stress of not meeting your rent or feeding your family. You need to put the money where it needs to go, take care of rent, safety, and security. Once you get that all paid for, you will realize you already have the love and belonging and self-esteem (that is the *Maz*, in Chapter 5) you need. That is success.

Rich People Have Everything – This is a myth. Rich people do not have everything, and they have lots of struggles. The other thing to consider is rich people and

---

64   The *Maz* puts things in order for you in Chapter 5—so you can live well and avoid harm, hunger, and homelessness.

smart people are **Normal**.[65] There are good ones and bad ones. Happy ones and not happy ones. Successful ones and not successful ones. There are rich people who are clueless, and there are rich people who are helpless. Rich people might have more of a safety net should they fail, but they can still go down the tubes if they do not understand what success is. They may not have the life experiences you do that allow you to keep going, to overcome, and to succeed. There is book smart, and there is life smart. Having either one is a gift that has to be used properly to increase the chances of success. Money can be taken away, but accomplishments cannot.

Money Buys Happiness – It turns out that after four or five years, lottery winners are not any happier than before they won the lottery. Life stayed **Normal**, and although the **Normal** shifted, there is still happiness and sadness. There is still disappointment. Bad things can still happen. They can still make bad decisions with their money. They can still have bad luck.

Marriage Is Bliss Forever – Marriage is generally awesome, but it is not always bliss. In one university study (we tried to avoid these but have to give credit where credit is due), it was found that after five to six years, married people thought they were less happy than they were before they were married.[66] Careful. The marriage is still happy, but people sometimes look at things the wrong way. This is why we get to know the **Kahn** in Chapter 8.

---

65 We mention **Normal** a lot. That is in Chapter 7. You might want to go back and read Chapters 2 and 3 first. If that seems like too much, try your timer out.

66 German Socio-Economic Panel, Clark, Diener and Georgellis in Kahneman, *Thinking, Fast and Slow*. Farrar, Straus and Giroux, New York, 2013. pp 398

In Chapter 8, we learn that we make a lot of judgments that are quick, efficient, but not necessarily accurate. Even the smartest of the smarty-pants make mistakes in their thinking and in their judgments. It is good to know that you can have some misconceptions about things, and then you know some of the mistakes you shouldn't make.

Learned Willfulness

By now you should realize you have the skills to move forward. Some people stop trying before they even get started. You need to watch out for any *learned helplessness*. Learned helplessness causes people to not even try or to quit before they even start. They are sure they are going to fail. Usually, they blame everyone else. "Why work if I am just going to be poor?" The *Kahn* teaches us that people who think they are losing take bad risks.[67]

Learned willfulness – Would you like to learn an act of learned willfulness? Do you have a smartphone? Let's not look at it and check our emails or our *social meds* for five minutes. Go to your timer. Set it for five minutes. Press start. Set down the phone. Go do something else until the timer goes off.

You willfully just made a small plan, a good decision, and we gave it some structure. That made it much easier to carry out. And you succeeded. Even if you had a random thought during the five minutes like "OMG, I wonder if Pooky-Bear is online! I better check." You generally can wait for four-and-a-half minutes—or consider getting a new Pooky-Bear.

Learning to get off your damn phone at work is extremely important. It is just fine to check it at coffee breaks and lunch breaks. You may find you enjoy life without stupid cat videos.

We want to learn willfulness. We want to learn how to behave so other people respect us and think we are cool. That idea has been around for a long time, and we let *Ari*[68] teach us how to find a *Moral Exemplar* (*M.E.*—someone to watch and to copy) and how to become an *M.E.* Check it out. You can avoid a lot of unpleasant situations by learning how to act. It is not acting stiff and formal; it is about willfully making good, small decisions in the workplace. We want to consciously make good things happen. We

---

67   Chapter 8, Math of *Kahn.*

68   Chapter 4, Getting to *Ari. Ari* is short for Aristotle, who was an ancient Greek philosopher.

want to consciously make small, positive decisions in the workplace like saying, "Thank you. I appreciate the help." Make a decision to ask a question and learn a little more about your job or about the *Org*.[69] Make a decision to ask people how long they have worked at *Org* and about their work history and make a decision to care about them.

Make small decisions like what you eat, what you drink, what you buy. Who you befriend, who you talk to, and who you follow on your *social meds*. When you sleep, when you learn, when you pray, when you exercise, and when you celebrate. Where you hang out, where you go, and where you relax. Understand that they are small decisions that you control, and at each point, you can make a good decision that will probably work in your favor, or you can make an obviously dumb-ass decision that will send you sliding down the *Pyramid* into crappy life river.

You are in control of what you learn, and you are in control of how you turn out—no matter what has happened up to this point. Make the effort to make it all happen.

Learning to Succeed

Learning is lifelong—enjoy. Start small. Use a timer. Repeat. Do you know how to go to a library? Try this. On a Saturday afternoon, go to a library. Just one Saturday. Go to a library. Open the door. Take a walk around the library. It's free. No one will talk to you. Although they may smile at you. You should feel safe. That is a sign of acceptance. Take your time. It is free. You can either pick out a book on something in particular that interests you (like basketball or history or pottery). Or you can go up to the counter and ask the person behind it to help you. Smile. You might find they are very helpful. Just a book. Remember where you got it from. Take it to a table. Sit down and open it. You do not have to read the whole thing. Just look through it. Read little parts that seem interest-ing or look at the pictures and what is written around them. Put the book back when you are done. Sit. Relax. Think. Maybe you want to take

---

69   Chapter 10 teaches you about the organization you work for. We refer to it as *Org* because you should treat it and the other people who work there as a living, breathing thing.

a pen and paper so you can write down some lists. Things I need, things I want, my to-do list for today or this week. Maybe my goals. You might want to have a notebook, or you can use this book as your notebook and write all over those weird empty pages at the back. Leave the library. Was it a good experience or a bad experience?

Saturday To-Do List

Wake up

Coffee

Healthy food

Shower

Clean up room (five minutes)

Clean up house (ten minutes)

Take out garbage

Walk/jog half a mile (ten minutes)

Library (thirty minutes)

Lunch (healthyish sorta)

Walk (twenty minutes)

_____

_____

_____

_____

Maybe just go out and look at other people. What is their life like? In Chapter 6 we talk about what makes up other people. It helps if you can figure out what fillings are in other people.

You might have been looking at school as your only way to measure whether you are succeeding—rocking the report card. Let's go find your success outside of school as well. Let's have a Saturday of successes. Like work, it is kind of a "by yourself" affair. Take the day. Use your timer. Do good things in small chunks. Start with a rough plan. Check out the start of a "Saturday To-Do List" on the previous page. Fill it out and go see how much more you can accomplish.

How did you make out? Did you have a successful day? So that is success. You set out to do something and you do most of it. Maybe it wasn't perfect, but you didn't do perfectly horribly either. Keep going. Try it again tomorrow. Maybe add some other things to your list, and knock off some long-term things you haven't gotten around to, like the following:

- Call or email someone who is not your bestie and say something nice.

- Willfully learn something.

- Do something physical.

- Clean up or organize something in your house.

- Create or update your budget for the week.

- Be the one to pick up a piece of trash and put it in the trash can, even if it isn't yours.

- Set some goals for the week.

Success doesn't mean you have to cure cancer, although we would appreciate it if you would. Here, success is a set of good decisions, even if they are small decisions. They are willful acts in that they are something good you set out to do, and you note they are not negative acts—like supporting organized crime, damaging property, or disrespecting authority.[70]

It is this success and this way of acting that will propel you to succeed in the workplace. We need small, ongoing, willful acts that help get the job done.[71] Small acts that are good for the organization.[72] Small acts that are good for your life.

Monsters

How many ACEs[73] do you have up your sleeve? Everyone has one or more. Some are really bad, and some are **Normal**. Everyone has a bad day in their past. For some, it was because they never got the blue pony they always wanted. For others, it involved the police, or family members seriously hurting each other. If you have a sleeve full of ACEs, or other monsters in your closet, we want to separate those out as best we can

---

70   Disagree with authority all you want. Don't disrespect it.

71   We talk more about the actual job and how to do it in Chapter 10.

72   We talk more about the actual organization (we call it **Org**), how it works, and what it needs in Chapter 10.

73   ACE – adverse childhood experience.

and leave them in the closet—shove them in the closet—while we go to work. The good thing about work is that as you rack up more successes, you become more about your successes and less about your ACEs. The hand you have been dealt will always be there. But we can make it less important and learn that it is a smaller piece of your *Pie* (Chapter 6).

As you get more successes, your brand[74] will improve. More people will know and respect you for the good things you do, for being reliable, and for being there to help them with their work life. This will increase your social capital (value), and you own it, it is real. The value of your stock goes up. You can use your social capital to get a better job or a better position within your company that pays a little more. Maybe they will send you for more training. Maybe after two or three years, they will put you on an airplane and fly you somewhere, all expenses paid, to go learn something, maybe even pay for your hotel and your food. Just so you can willfully get even better for your organization.

Coming Home

Your family may have only armed you with fear, stress, anxiety, and anger. You have to reprogram you for the workplace. You may have a fight-or-flight habit that is very ingrained in you (and makes up a big piece of your *Pie*). When people flee a situation, they are heading for an exit. Maybe they are heading for safety. Maybe they are just fleeing life. If you are always heading towards the exit, you are seldom choosing the right door. Once the exit door slams you on the butt on your way out, it is really hard to go back in. Don't exit. Stay. We need you.

If your family is full of issues, bad issues, then it may be up to you to empower yourself to take care of you first, and then take care of them with whatever you have left over. You cannot do it from the middle of poop river. If you have a sleeve full of ACEs, try to stay close to shore. Maybe the workplace is just the place to keep the poop from getting

---

74   Think of yourself as a thing for a moment. Would most people want to buy? Do you have good features? Or will you break down and make a mess on the floor? Just like a computer or a dishwasher? Or toilet paper? Do you get the job done?

inside your boots. Work is generally much safer. You may find you want to hang out there.

If you think there are lots of stupid adults out there, you might be right. A lot of us agree with you. You can be smarter than them, and that can help you get ahead and stay away from harm, hunger, and homelessness.

Finally

None of this is easy. But you are strong enough to get this far. You have what it takes to go far but you may want a compass and a roadmap. You will find (or have already found) the direction in the rest of the chapters. That direction will take you further away from harm, hunger, and homelessness.

You can live with decent finances, family, and friends—for the health of it. Maybe the other parts of this book are worth reading to help strengthen and organize the skills you already have. They can help you get a valuable job and be valuable at your job, and maybe you can end up **Golden**.

You got the skills. We are all cheering for you. Quietly.

CHAPTER 12
Wealth Killers

You had a lot of skills when you started your journey through this book, and now you have more. You have the skills to do great in the workplace—get a good job, advance in the company or move to a higher position in another company, get more training related to your job to make more money. All the skills have

been building the positive side of your **Pyramid**, helping you get better traction to climb up that slope. Your **Pie** is looking bigger, your slice of the **Pie** is bigger, and maybe it has some whipped cream on top. You are ready to make more **Pennies**. But you can always screw up.

We have purposefully stayed away from throwing "university studies" or other data at you. You are smart enough to understand people can make statistics fit what they want them to fit. This section makes sense on its own. No geeks from universities required. There are people whom I respect greatly: **Ari** sat on a rock and thought about how humans should act; the **Maz** didn't study economics, or finance—he just thought about what people need to take care of to make things better for themselves; the **Kahn** didn't find two zillion ways of thinking—he found two. Let's think about the things that can screw up your work life. Let's be honest. Life can be pretty simple.

You can make decisions that either shrink your **Pie**, shrink your piece of your **Pie**, or cause you to lose all of your **Pennies**. With all of these, you lose. So, make better decisions. Here are five wealth killers served along with some brutal honesty. Some of these you absolutely control; some you have a lot of control over. Some of this is **Normal**. Go through life with eyes wide open.

There are five wealth killers.

1. Drugs

2. Unemployment

3. Single parenthood

4. Divorce

5. Child support

Remember, this is about your work life. This is not about your religious or moral considerations. What you decide or how you make good decisions is up to you. What is right and wrong is up to you. We can respect each other even if we do not 100 percent agree on every single aspect of our lives. If you want to have a reasonably good adulthood most of the time (because life is *Normal*), then you better not let these five things bite you in the ass. It should be quite simple to start with *Ari's Golden Mean*, and then do well from there. But bad is bad.

There is a bright side to all of this. Other people will screw up. If you don't screw up, you get to step aside while they are sliding down their *Pyramid*, leaving more room for you in the higher elevations. If you can avoid the wealth killers, you likely get a higher spot on the *Pyramid*, closer to a bit of time singing *Kumbaya* with *Pennies* jingling in your bank account. If you bypass these pitfalls, you will definitely be further away from harm, hunger, and homelessness. Consider that as you read below.

Drugs

We are talking about either drugs that are illegal and harm you and everyone around you, or drugs that are legal that mostly harm you and the people who love you. With respect to drug use and the workplace, there are two issues: drug use and drug testing.

Drug Use

You can't function at work on drugs, and no one wants to work with you if you are on or using drugs. No one wants to prop up your sorry ass 'cuz you are high or you are hanging. No one should have to cover for you because you can't contribute to the work family. This is one instance where a family can boot your sorry ass out on your sorry ass. Sorry, not sorry.[75]

It goes a little further than that. Our society is a little more complex these days than a hundred years ago. There was only so much damage you could do if you were stoned while digging a ditch with a shovel in your hand. Ya, you suck for the day, but there are a hundred other people digging the same ditch and just because you suck, they are still digging, and you probably can't really hurt anyone. Those days have passed.

Today, we have a lot of really expensive equipment that can get messed up. No one wants to let some Jackwagon (or Jillwagon) near a three-hundred-thousand-dollar piece of equipment if they were high ten hours ago. No one wants to worry about you causing an accident and hurting someone because you are too wasted or too hung to pay attention. No one wants to inform your family that you hurt yourself or someone else on the job. Maybe it is just causing a problem with the French fry machine; maybe you delete a bunch of information on the computer that everyone needs; maybe you fall asleep and your crew doesn't meet its goal. Maybe you burn someone with hot oil at the French fry machine or kill a family while driving a company vehicle.

It goes a little further than that. Illegal drugs go hand in hand with organized crime. If you use illegal drugs, if you buy illegal drugs, if you sell illegal drugs, if you sell legal drugs illegally, you are hand in hand with organized crime that participates in human trafficking, sex slavery, terrorism, murder, financial crimes, and so on. Nice company you keep. People in the workplace do not want any part of you. They want to lead their nice *Normal* lives and be an accepted part of the work family. They

---

75 You can always use that great skill of procrastinating to avoid drugs. Put it off. Just not today. Maybe tomorrow. Repeat.

want a decent chance of a nice piece of *Pie* on their *Pyramid* with a few *Pennies* in their pocket. They don't want to deal with that other crap.

Goldilocks doesn't need you ruining everyone's day because you are screwed up. *Goldilocks* needs everything from you just right, even if you are just entering your time into the computer so you can get paid, or you are checking in stuff that is received. *Goldilocks* needs their information, and they need you to keep up your end of your bargain and get your stuff done safely, correctly, legibly, and on time. If you can't come to work with a reasonably clear mind, then you are going to face a steeper climb up a smaller *Pyramid* and have to work harder, all for a smaller piece of *Pie*. The higher levels of your *Pyramid* will be closed for the rest of the season.

Drugs have no place in the workplace or among the work family. End of story.

Drug Testing

Over half of American employers (56 percent[76]) require you to pass a drug test before they will employ you. They pay out over 3.7 billion dollars on drug testing every year, for all the reasons mentioned above, and more. If you want to reduce your chance of success in your career, then consider you can't work for half of the employers in the US if you can't pass a drug test. You should also realize that the half of employers that require you to be clean are the ones that pay better and provide better benefits. Hopefully, you can make that connection in your brain. Table 12.1 is a very, very small sample of companies that perform drug testing.[77]

---

76   https://www.psychemedics.com/blog/2018/01/surprising-stats-drugs-workplace/

77   https://www.testclear.com/dtcompanies/companyresults.aspx

Table 12.1 – Small Sample of Companies That Screen Employees for Drug Use

Transportation

USA Cartage, FedEx, United Parcel Service, Ryder, Kuehne & Nagel

Banks and finance

GE Capital, Bank of America, Household Finance, American Express, US Bank, Fidelity

Vehicle rental

Enterprise, Zipcar, Penske, Budget, Avis, Hertz

Communications

Comcast, Verizon, Sprint, Dish Network

Construction

Vulcan Materials, Granite Construction, Oldcastle, Hubbard, Martin Marrietta

Chemicals

US Polymers, AkzoNobel, Chemical Lime, Cargill, Lubrizol, Ingevity, ICL, Westlake, Proctor & Gamble, PPG Industries, Dow, Dupont

Department of Defense

Air Force, Navy, Army, Marines

Food and Beverage

Hershey, Pepsi, Coca-Cola, Coors, Anheuser Busch, Miller, Robert Mondavi, Kraft, Conagra

Retail

Ikea, Target, Walmart, Costco, Sam's Club, Safeway, Publix, Best Buy, Walgreens, Home Depot, Kohls, Lowes, Kroger, Barnes & Noble, Staples

Oil

Marathon, Valero, Exxon, Tesoro, PBF Energy, Shell Oil, Suncor, Chevron, Mobil

Tires

Cooper, Goodyear, Bridgestone

Technology

Microsoft, US Computer, Lenovo, Magna, Hewlett-Packard, NXP Semiconductor, Amazon, AOL, Nintendo, Oracle, Xerox

Vehicle makers

Fiat-Chrysler, BMW, Toyota, General Motors, Harley Davidson

Railroad

UP, BNSF, Amtrak, Genesee & Wyoming

Forestry

Georgia Pacific, Universal Forestry Products, Weyerhauser, Canfor

Restaurants

Cracker Barrel, Denny's, Hooters, McDonalds, Pizza Hut, Mortons, Round Table, Jack in the Box, Burger King, Dominoes, Taco Bell

Oilfield Services

Schlumberger, Baker Hughes, Halliburton

Utilities

PG&E, Ameren, Duke Energy

Metals and Materials

Alcoa, Tremco, Nucor Yamato Steel, Inland Cement

Pharmaceuticals

Pfizer, Merck, Bayer, Eli Lilly

Health

Signa, Allegiant, Blue Shield, United Healthcare, Clarion, Bayfront Health, Cigna, Humana, Mercy Health, Healthcare

Airlines

Alaska, American, Air Canada

Insurance

Geico, Aegon, Progressive, Prudential, State Farm

Hotels

Hilton, Marriott, Palms Hotel & Casino, Ritz Carlton, Westin, Harrah's

We are not going to bother going into some Internet fantasy about how you can use and then mask your use. Sorry, that is a lousy strategy that will fail. Also, only the simplest tests don't pick up the masking chemicals. The same companies that are screening you before they hire also require random testing while at work in order to maintain your employment. In the last twenty years, even in senior management, I have come to expect three to four random drug tests per year. It is annoying and bothersome. There have been days I wish they had meeting rooms at the drug clinic, because there are a bunch of us there and we may as well be useful. But successful people don't get angry about drug testing for obvious reasons—we avoid drugs and people who use drugs.

Workplace Accidents

If you are involved in a workplace accident, you can expect a drug test. You do not necessarily have to be at fault. If you are involved in an accident with the general public while you are working, and there is property damage or injuries, then the **Org** is going to want to make sure there is no liability. Lawyers will try anything to sue **Org**. If **Org** can supply clean drug tests for the people involved (you), the other party is going to have a harder time getting money from **Org**. If it is a workplace accident, **Org** wants to protect you and the workers around you. They send everyone involved for drug tests to ensure they are providing a clean and safe workplace. If you fail the drug test, you are fired.

If you fail a drug test, you can expect to be fired for employee misconduct. In most states, this means you will not be eligible for unemployment insurance. Unemployment insurance is intended for those who lose their job through no fault of their own. You don't have to take the drug test if you don't want to—you just have to go work somewhere else. And somewhere else is getting harder and harder to find. So maybe don't live a life that fails the drug test.

Moral Considerations

The workplace doesn't care about your moral considerations. You may be morally superior to me and everyone else who has read this book, and thus you should be able to do whatever you want with your body—absolutely correct. Go do what you want. We just don't need to work with you if you are on or using drugs. We really don't want to hang out with you, and we are not interested in getting to know you; you are an embarrassment to your family. Well done. We hope that you are enjoying the moral high horse you are on. Hope you find a way to buy your horse some oats. Good jobs will be hard to come by.

It doesn't matter if drugs are legal. This is about the workplace and safety, not about your rights. Do what you want; we just don't have to have you in the workplace.

OK, but you are the receptionist not operating anything dangerous, or you work totally by yourself and always get your work done. Fair enough. But the law says the **Org** has to treat everyone in the workplace the same. Can't play favorites. We can't just drug-test the dudes and dudettes who do the really dangerous stuff. No, if we test one, we have to test all. Fair is fair. It is the moral thing to do.

Common Drug Tests

There are two common types of drug tests in the work world: the urine test and the hair test. Either of these can be used for employment screening to

a. avoid hiring drug users who are more likely to cause accidents and to bring harm to the other staff and to **Org**, and

b. catch employees who are using drugs while employed and who are more likely to cause accidents and to harm the other staff and harm **Org**.

Let's look at each one.

1. Urine Analysis

The good old pee test requires good aim and a steady hand and gives the employer a quick look at whether the pee-er was using drugs within the last two to three days. Random tests should happen on Mondays, but they don't. They can happen any day of the week. It will likely take a couple of hours, and you get paid while you get your drug test.

Generally, for a random test, you will be tested either on-site or off-site—it depends on the company you are working for. You might be given an address of a drug testing clinic to go to and you are expected to head there either immediately, or within twenty-four hours. It is like going to a doctor's office. When you arrive at the facility and check-in, they will ask you for photo ID. They will ask you for your purse, your backpack, and everything in your pockets. They want to make sure you are not smuggling in someone else's pee. (Wow—who would do that?)

You will be shown to a private, secure bathroom and given a sample container to pee in. Just like in a doctor's office. Once you fill it up, you hand it in or leave it in the bathroom, and the staff will take it and seal it. It is all done very professionally, very privately.

The results will be sent to the human resources department at *Org*. You generally will never hear about the results. Unless you fail.

2. Hair Test

A hair test is a great way to start a new fashion trend. Even though you may read they only take one hundred to two hundred strands, it can be a larger sample. I had a half-inch bald spot across the back four inches of my head. I wore a hat for a few days. A hair test typically identifies drug use for the past ninety days or more. It is more comprehensive and usually used more for pre-employment screening.

If you choose to be bald, they will take hair from wherever hair grows on your body. If you are completely denuded of hair that is your right. But no hair sample, no job.

If you have a medical condition that causes you lose all your body hair (a real condition called *alopecia universalis*, or AU), you will likely need a letter from a doctor and an understanding **Org**.

Hair tests are more expensive to conduct than urine tests, so they are generally done for higher-paying or riskier jobs. If you are starting out in the workplace, you may not be subjected to the cheap haircut.

Your rights are paramount at any drug-screening facility. Your privacy is absolutely upheld. You will get to pee in your own cup in a little private room, just like a doctor's office. It is an adult thing to do. It is always a little stressful, even when you are clean. One of those **Normal** events in life. If you are fired for a failed drug test, it may follow you around for your career. But once you pass the drug test, you are in. In a workplace club that is further away from harm, hunger, and homelessness. It's where the cool kids hang out.

We have talked about procrastinating throughout the book. Put off doing drugs just like cleaning your room. Just for today. Repeat tomorrow. Now you have a real reason. Look at it this way. Lots of successful people don't do drugs. Lots of people who do drugs are not successful. Which one of those groups do you want to be in? Employment is one of the best excuses to not do drugs.

Unemployment

At some point in your career, you are going to be unemployed. Likely you are right now. Maybe someone is paying all your expenses right now, and you do not need much to live on. At some point, you may have kids to pay for, a house, a car, credit cards, food, heat, a boat, ballet lessons, school, and shoes you just had to have. Etcetera. Unemployment can hit you out of nowhere, or maybe you see it coming. Maybe you are just between jobs. Hopefully, you have some money tucked away so you can cover your *Maz* for a while on your own. Hopefully, you are not living at or beyond your limit. Hopefully, your credit cards are used for convenience, not because you do not have money in your bank account.

As soon as your earnings are zero, you are not creating wealth; you are destroying wealth. Maybe not yours right away, but you are taking away someone's wealth. Every penny counts.

It takes longer to get a job than you think. We look at the process in Chapter 14. We are almost there.

There is a thing called *unemployment insurance*[78] in both the US and Canada. It is only intended for workers who lose their job through no fault of their own. If you are fired for not showing up, failing a drug test, breaking company rules, insubordination, or simply being a lousy worker, there is no unemployment insurance. Here is a tip: Unemployment insurance is to tide you over, so you need to get back to work. You need to work as soon as possible. Unemployment insurance is not free money.

There are lots of places to go on the Internet to read about unemployment insurance if you want. It varies depending on where you live. Here are the basics:

1. You must work long enough to be eligible for unemployment.

2. It does not last forever. Usually, if you are fully qualified (like you have been working for a few years), you are eligible for up to

---

78   Insurance is something you have that provides some protection against a loss. It rarely completely covers your loss. Only some. No matter what kind of insurance you are talking about.

twenty-six weeks. That may sound like a lot, but it is only meant to tide you over until you get another job and another income. It doesn't replace all of your income. It varies, but it is generally 60 to 70 percent of what you were making. It replaces somewhere from $40 to $450 per week. (If you are working forty hours per week, you may expect $450, or about $11.25 per hour.)

3. It will take a bit of time to kick in, and it will take some time to get the money, so you need to have some money tucked away to tide you over. Think about that when you are saving a little money so you can pay the rent.

It takes four to six weeks to get a job and get your first paycheck. Even the simplest, most basic job takes time. Application process, interview, pre-employment screening, background test, drug screening—it all takes time.

Every time you are between jobs, you are not climbing; you are hanging on. Hanging on consumes energy and resources. If you are always between jobs, then you have nothing left. You are not growing. You are on the sidelines, sidelined.

"Hi, I'm nothing. I do not do anything. I have nothing to contribute." This is not a good opening line when you are trying to meet people. Unemployment happens to lots of people. It is hard to stay on the love and belonging floor or the self-esteem floor of your **Pyramid** if you are unemployed. It is a tough period for most people to go through. There is no magic answer. Go back to the basics and get **Golden** and start your climb again. Maybe you got bad lucky, or maybe you were bad.

You may have to have more than one job to replace the one job you just lost. Hopefully, it is temporary until you get your **M.E.** back and start to climb back up your **Maz**.

Single Parenthood

Juan Williams, an author and journalist, lays out four traits to be successful in his book *Enough*.

1. Finish high school.

2. Get and keep a job.

3. Get married only after you have finished high school and have a job.

4. Only have children if you are over twenty-one and have a job.

I respect Mr. Williams greatly but think people are better off if they wait until they are twenty-five or older to start making kids. I don't care if you practice. There is no hurry to have kids. Yes, you are an adult. Kids need adults for parents. Not brand-new shiny adults. Adults with a few miles on them. The better your *Maz* is, the better parent you can become. Kids are awesome—having them is not a race. Being in your twenties is awesome; it is not a race. You need to make sure you and your partner can stand being on the same planet for the long haul. You want to make sure you and your partner really like each other before you bring another life onto this planet.

Parenting is a challenge that will expand to take all the physical, emotional, and financial resources you have. You need a spouse to help you with parenting, or at least a spouse who goes out and makes a bunch of money to throw into the family *Maz*. You still have a lot of growing to do. Waiting a few years for kids may seem like it takes a long time, but it can be time that lets you move to the area you want to live in, live in the home you want to raise your children in, and be the adult parent you want to be.

Single parenting is not the best way to parent. It is unfair to the kids. It is unfair to you. Yes, a village can raise a child—along with two loving parents. The parents come first—then the village can help. Single parenting will keep you and your kids in a continual struggle against the lowest level of your *Maz*. No one is keeping you down; you have kept yourself down. Kids are expensive financially, emotionally, and logistically. It is a bitch trying to do it yourself, so why would you bother? How is it fair to your kid?

Babies, Booze, and Drugs

Now that girls and boys are equal, there are two equally stupid sides to the equation when it comes to having children out of wedlock and before having life partners or before throwing your graduation cap in the air. Now, both girls and guys drink too much and do stupid things and make babies through some drunken, drugged-up haze. Not cool. Not mature. Not adult. Then it is unlikely the mother can get through pregnancy without drinking and drugging herself and harming the way-more-important, little, defenseless creature she is baking in her tummy. Girls act just as dumb as guys now (yay, progress) and drink much more than they used to. This—and having nookie—leads to more kids being born with fetal alcohol issues that are lifelong. It doesn't take much to affect the little fetus for their entire life. If you are going to be boinking, even with protection, you have to consider the possibility of a little you being created. Until you know you are not pregnant, you are pregnant. No booze, no drugs. Or you are an idiot.[79] Definitely not Golden.

The booze goes through the placenta (the little baby sac) as easy as you swallowed it down your gullet. Neither is pretty. Even mild exposure can cause a great little kid to have to deal with learning issues their entire life (and you and the teachers will bear the brunt of dealing with those issues). Issues include learning math, money, and time. They may also have social difficulties with friendship, and learning barriers—like sitting still, not sitting on stranger's laps, and keeping hands to themselves in school and on the playground. Coordination and athletics are stunted. ADHD is so common we are not even going to define it.

---

79   The art of procrastinating is discussed a couple times. Put it off today. Repeat.

The difference between kids who are born clean and healthy and those who are born with drugs in their system or who have been exposed to alcohol in the womb is huge. Huger than you think. Can you imagine that the little brain has holes in its existence because Mom was drinking and partying while she was pregnant? It is a very big deal. It's majorly unfair to bring kids into the world without two parents, or with parents who have substance issues. The kid is going to fight a tough battle throughout school and beyond trying to learn, trying to understand, and trying to relate to what is going on around them. Even if they might seem really funny and really social, it may be all part of the big jumble in their tiny brain. So be smart. Don't bring kids into this world until you are ready to give your entire, silly-assed life to being a parent. It is not a part-time hobby. It takes every bit of you and your partner.

Don't misread this. This is not directed at single Moms. They didn't do it alone. If you are the dad, then man up, the kid matters more than you. We like the kid more than you. You need to be around. That kid is going to be awesome, and you are just going to end up old and ugly anyhow. At least the kid and the Mom might like you.

As soon as that child is created, as soon as that child is born, it is more important than you are. You might need to grow up before you can really live with that. You will no longer (or should no longer) have time to always look your best or head out with your tribe every weekend. It just can't happen. There is laundry and feedings and teething and a lot of dirty diapers. Two of you will need to stay home—or you will certainly need to understand what matters when you do go out.

There is zero excuse for getting pregnant if you are not married. There is zero excuse for putting a child into a single-parent home. Bringing a child into the world with only a single parent is a childish thing for anyone to do. You have just shown you are not mature if you are not mature enough to take steps to not create a child before you are emotionally, physically, and financially ready.

Zero excuse. Both of you.

And very costly.

Divorce

Marriage and having kids are two of life's events that provide the upper levels of your *Maz* (self-esteem and self-actualization), regardless of your career or your education or your address. Most of us are wired to want a family and all that comes with it, even if we can't put our finger on what "it" actually is. Marriage is a lifelong commitment to be better than the sum of your parts, and you will have more than the sum of your parts. Marriage is also an investment that grows and grows. It is not necessarily a straight line, and it will be more *Normal* than you may wish. You will get back more than you can imagine from being married, and unlike most things you buy, marriage gets stronger and better-looking the longer you have it. Sadly, you can always screw up.

If you can't screw up your own life enough, you can always have some kids and then toss them off their little **Pyramids**. Nice parenting. Kids deserve two parents who love and respect each other. How else are they supposed to grow and turn into the adults we want them to turn into? Sure, they might turn out okay in a single-parent family. But how do they learn how they should be treated or how they treat someone if they do not see it in front of them daily? Remember, marriage is *Normal*. Sometimes after five or six years, some people think they are less happy than they were before they got married. Forget the bliss of the first few years. That has worn off.

Marriage is not just about Mommy and Daddy being in bliss for the rest of their lives. This is about how you keep your *Maz* as a family. This is about how you share the work that has to be done, and how you work together to keep growing the stash of *Pennies* and making the *Pie* a little bigger for the whole family. There can be no win in divorce, even it is one of the fluffy-peace-and-love divorces. The total amount of money the family makes is the same. Mommy and Daddy might make the same amount of money the day after the family gets flushed down the sewer. But now there are two households to pay for. Expenses went way up, and income is the same—or soon to be lower. If we look at the family *Pyramid*, the cost of safety and security went way up (you have two homes to pay for instead of one), so the money available for love and belonging and for self-esteem must go way down. Logistics and transportation just took a much larger slice of the *Pie*. Now there is twenty minutes of travel time to go pick up a kid and take them to their ball practice or their dance lesson. Each way. More money on gas, less time to yourself, less time with your kids. At best. Who is winning in this? Whose *Pie* is getting better? Who is getting more money to improve the family's *Maz*? How do you not slide down your *Pyramid*?

There was some crap about how children of divorce turn out just fine—kids are resilient. OK. Sure. Let's pose a question. Is it all right if someone comes up and punches your kid in the face? Just once? Why not? Kids are resilient. Oh, so even if they are resilient, we still don't want to see them hurt. Their resilience is not an excuse to blow up their family and slide them on down the *Pyramid*. Don't make your *Normal* little life problems become their whole life problems. You just $%^#ed their *Golden* foundation.

There are real reasons for divorce. Violence and abuse, for example. If the kids are getting ACEs up their sleeves, then you deserve a pass outta' there. But if your spouse isn't your spicy piece of *Pie* any longer—oh, well. Sucks to be you. Marriage is *Normal*. Blooms fall off roses—they don't last forever. If you are thinking marriage is forever Nirvana, you are wrong. Marriage is great, marriage is wonderful—marriage is not perfect. Marriage does get better with time, and it does get stronger after you get over every *Normal* setback—as long as both parties are putting their best efforts into the marriage and the family.

Your marriage is going to be *Normal*, like your life is going to be *Normal*. You want it to be the best *Normal* it can be. But it's *Normal*. It has good days and not-so-good days. There will be some really bad days. There will be awesome, inspiring days. There will be a lot of dirty socks and underwear. And bathrooms that smell like a garbage dump. Hopefully, you two end up really good, very deep friends who care very deeply for each other, and get the joy only having grown kids and grandkids can give you. You can build the ultimate solid *Pyramid* that you can pass to your kids and set them up to build their own. Because when you are both seventy and naked, you are both going to look like sacks of cottage cheese in nylons. Soft light will be your friend.

If you break up your family, the *Pennies* that used to pay for one home now have to pay for two homes. Worse, the *Pennies* now have to set up a second home with furniture, microwaves, beds, TVs, washers and dryers—the very things that sucked the finances down the tube in the beginning of the marriage. If there was financial pressure before you divvied up your kid's life, it will be excruciating when you decide to go chasing your blue pony.[80] Surprise, surprise, your partner may not think too highly of you for deciding to flush the family. They may get a lawyer, and then you will both lose everything. You now take the same amount of money, give most of it to a lawyer, and then set up two homes. Even if you win, everyone loses. But at least you get to go back to trying to look like you're twenty-one and acting like an ass (yay, equality). You can go get a new partner who has a whole new set of flaws. The socks, underwear, and bathroom will still be the biological warzone. Well done.

You can see an example in Table 12.2. Here is a family that is doing well, is making one hundred thousand dollars per year, and has two kids. One or both parents decide to go chasing blue ponies and tank the kids' family.

Assume you are in California and are paying child support for two kids. You make five thousand dollars per month (sixty thousand dollars per year), and your partner makes thirty-five hundred dollars (forty-two thousand dollars per year). You can expect to pay about $1,096 per month in child support. The state takes about a third of your income for taxes. We will assume the parent who makes more money has to pay the parent who makes less money. Assuming the kid(s) go to live with the parent who made less . . .

---

80   Do you need a blue pony? Exactly. Why chase it?

Table 12.2 – Family Finance and Divorce

	Parent 1	Parent 2	Total	Parent 1 After Child Support	Parent 2 After Child Support
Annual Income	$60,000	$42,000	$102,000		
Monthly Income	$5,000	$3,500	$8,500	$5,000	$3,500
Taxes	($1,665)	($1,155)	($2,820)	($1,665)	($1,155)
Child Support				($1,100)	$1,100
Net Income	$3,335	$2,245	$5,580	$2,235	$3,455
% Change in Take-Home Pay				Decrease 33 %	Increase 54%

Both parents had $5,580 to pay for the family's Maz. After the breakup and now paying child support, even though one is paying and one is receiving, they make $2,235 and $3,445 separately to pay for their Maz. Child support solves nothing. Now the kid(s) are living in a home with 35% less money than prior to the breakup ($ 3,455 after vs. $ 5,580 before). That oughtta work.

Combined, the parents bring home $5,580 per month, after taxes, and look after one home. Now the $5,580 per month to pay for the family's Maz is reduced to $3,445 per month in the main home where the kids live. There is only $2,235 in the other home. How is this better? Go back and check out the *Pyramid*, or the money *Pie*. Most of the money goes to paying for a home (rent or mortgage), so how are you going to pay for two homes on the same income?

Divorce will kill wealth by increasing costs and reducing income. The money is no longer used as efficiently and everyone will lose. The kids will not get access to the same level of activities because single parents have a hard-enough time getting enough money to pay the bills.

So you screw up your *Maz*, shrink your *Pie*, and lose your *Pennies*. So you can get a new set of flaws to grind your teeth over?

And child support? Oh goody, let's see how that looks.

Child Support

The things they do not tell you about in school. Here is a very straightforward approach to child support. If you get tagged for child support, you have to pay child support. End of story.

The meter starts ticking and it does not shut off. The meter might go back to the moment when the kid was born, and that might be years ago. You may not have even known it happened. You might get tagged with a bill that has been growing like a dust bunny under your bed. If you get tagged, you get tagged. The amount you owe is never forgiven. If you do not keep up on your payments, you are in *arrears*. They can show up on your credit report, there is no way out. Consider all of that when you are heading out on the weekend.

You can be tagged for child support if you are the biological parent, or if you are a stepparent and there is no biological parent in the picture.[81] The single parent, who is likely hurting for money, is going to get it wherever they can. The court is going to help them. They are going to find money to help raise the child, even if there is no way of knowing if the child is going to benefit from the money.

If you are ordered to pay child support and you refuse, your former partner can go to court and get an injunction to have money deducted by **Org** directly from your paycheck. **Org** will deduct the money from your check and submit it to the proper government agency. **Org** doesn't have a choice in the matter. **Org** will not break the law on your behalf, because then they will owe the money. This is called having your wages *garnisheed*. There is no forgiveness. If you are working two jobs to get ahead, the court may get you at both jobs—whatever the court needs to get the money you owe for child support. They may take extra if you are in arrears.

---

81   The courts refer to it as *loco parentis*. It means *in place of a parent*. If you have been being a great person and helping someone raise their child, you can still get tagged for child support. Even if it is not biologically yours. Even if there was no agreement between you and your partner regarding their kid.

It's not the kid's fault. If you are paying, it sucks to be you. As soon as you parent a child, the child is more important than you. Consider all of that when you are heading out for the weekend.

If you are paying child support and you lose your job, or you make less money because you take a lesser job, you may still be tagged for the original amount. If you were working two jobs, and now you only have time to work one, because you need visitation time, you can still be charged child support as if you were still working two jobs. So if you were making sixty thousand dollars per year (about thirty dollars per hour), and then you have to take a lesser job for whatever reason, you may still be on the hook for child support at the sixty-thousand-dollars-per-year level. This is called *imputed income*. The court will make you pay support on your *capacity to earn money*, not the money you actually earn. If you once made sixty thousand dollars per year, then you should be able to make that money again. Keep paying. Even if you can no longer make that money because of all the inefficiencies in your **Maz** now that you are paying for children you do not live with.

Child support does not end on the child's eighteenth birthday. It can keep going until the child finishes whatever schooling they decide to go to after high school. You can be on the hook even if the child's parent remarries or you remarry. The court will not care about how many kids you have. The court wants as much money as possible for the kid even if you think the money is just being wasted on things other than the kid.

That sex partner, whom you may have spent ten years or ten minutes with, has people behind them urging them to go for all the child support they can. Don't expect sympathy from anyone. The child is more important than you are. Consider all of that when you are heading out for the weekend.

Summary

Life is **Normal**, and you can expect to hit some obstacles on the way. We are tremendously lucky to live where we do. We live in the safest, most prosperous country in the world, **Normally**. The opportunities for us to avoid harm, hunger, and homelessness are huge. We have to be aware of what to avoid so we don't put our foot, or our children's feet, in a steaming pile of life crap. Drugs, unemployment, and bad relationships are the sorts of things that take decades off your ability to pay your **Maz**, to enjoy a good-sized **Pie**, and to always have some **Pennies** in your pocket.

You know all of this. Does any of it really surprise you? You probably decided early in the book to be **Golden** and to be your own **M.E.** Awesome. Please do. We need your help.

CHAPTER 13

You and Your Job

We have spent a lot of time laying the foundation for you to do great things at work. The workplace will provide more than money. It builds your **Maz** and supplies most of your **Pie**. The workplace is the arena for you to step in and shine—even if you step in right smack dab in the middle with your **Mean**ness. The workplace will allow you to be the **M.E.** you want to be. If you make reasonably good decisions with your **Pennies** (basing those decisions on your **Maz**) and you get **Golden** with your **Mean**, you will likely have mostly great days. Need we say they will be great or **Normal?** You will meet your goal of avoiding harm, hunger, and homelessness. Boom.

Your job will be an intersection of you and your employer (see Figure 13.1).

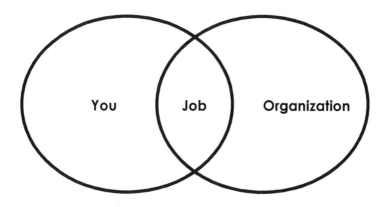

Figure 13.1 – You and Your Job

This intersection is your opportunity to build your **Pyramid** and collect your **Pennies.** Whether you are starting a six-week internship or you are starting in a Wall Street law firm, the intersection matters. The organization has to matter to you, or you are disrespecting all the other people who have poured their life's work into building the organization. What those other people have built is what is going to allow you to come in and have a job. And they want your help. Help them and you will be *Golden*.

How much a part of you, and how big a part of *Org*, how big your job is will vary over your life. To get started, you are well advised to make your job an important part of your life. It may not be that way every day, as life happens—births, weddings, funerals, and so on. *Org* and your co-workers understand that—it is *Normal*. *Org* and your co-workers want your help, they need you to participate. You give them an honest effort, and you will be surprised how much you are appreciated by your co-workers, and you will receive lots from them for your effort. Remember the goal: Avoid harm, hunger, and homelessness. If you want to be *Golden*, if you want to be on the right side of *Normal*, you are going to take the job seriously, put your ass into your job, and cool your coolness.

Every job is going to have four parts that you have to attend to. And every job has one children's character to attend to (their name is *Goldilocks*).

The four parts of every job are:

- Duties
- Administration
- Data
- Communication

Let's look at each one.

Duties

A company hires you to do something. Maybe clean floors, cure cancer, fight crime, or stick needles into people. Maybe you will put doohickey things on thingamajigs. Maybe they hire you to enter data in a computer or change the oil in cars. OK, great. There is much more to it, and companies haven't necessarily evolved to where they can tell you exactly what to do every second of the workday. You are an adult and expected to perform your job with maturity, professionalism, and integrity. You are expected to figure out some of these things for yourself, and you should have fun while you do it.

Many new employees walk in making a mistake as soon as they put a foot through the doorway. They are judged quickly, efficiently, not necessarily accurately. They are under the mistaken

Integrity is doing the right thing when no one is looking.

impression that they are just there to do a job. How **Golden** is that? Where is the **M.E.** in that? Mr./Ms. Grumpy B. Poopypants comes shuffling through the door either right at the time they are supposed to start or a few minutes after (because they are more important than the job). They don't make eye contact with anyone or say anything, and they take their long face all the way back to the change room so they can get out to their station ten minutes late and grace everyone with their coolness. "Yay," screamed no one, ever.

Entry-level jobs may sound basic, but they require you to integrate with a team inside of **Org**, or at the least, to participate with customers. If you are hired to sweep floors, then the expectation is you can arrive a couple of minutes before your shift, say "Hi" to people, maybe ask them about their day. Get yourself ready so that you start your task at the appointed time and place. Many places begin the day with a group meeting, a shift meeting, or a safety meeting. Once **Org** is paying you, you are part of **Org** and your phone is not. Your friends are not part of **Org**. Even if you are sitting in a coffee room waiting for the shift leader, be engaged with **Org**. Surfing your phone is the last thing you should do. For the first couple of weeks, browse through the employee manual, sit quietly while the experienced staff chats, or stand there with your hands in your pockets and just listen. Speak pleasantly when spoken to. Sitting and listening attentively shows the experienced staff you take them and **Org** seriously. You can ponder where the other staff is in their **Pyramid**, you can cut up their **Pie** in your head (10 percent old, 20 percent experienced, 40 percent mean . . .). There are lots of ways to while away the time while you are waiting. Checking out, not being attentive, or being too cool because you are scared to show weakness will not show you as the

Mean you that you are trying to be. When all else fails, be *Mean*. Think *Mean*, it will be *Normal*. It will get you to *Golden*.

Here is a list of things you need to accomplish to be successful in doing your duties:

1. **Do your job.** Too many new staff think they should go straight to the top. Oh, you brilliant summer college students that are so smart: You may be getting educated but whether you are smart or not, only time will tell. Do the job you were asked to do, even if you think you should be in the president's seat and queen of the world. Suck it up, buttercup, and sweep the floor if that is what you are asked to do, or better yet, even if you are not.

2. **Do your job safely.** For you and for me. No one wants to tell the family that little Poopsy just scarred themselves for life with acid or cut their thumb off with box cutters or ran someone over with the company vehicle because they were texting with their BFF.

3. **Obey the law.** Do not break the law for you or for the company's sake. No one wants you to. You are not doing anyone any favors; you are likely putting everyone at risk. Potentially, you put the owner(s) in jeopardy because you cut a corner or you thought you were going to save the company some money or you were breaking a rule because it was easier for you. You are Type 1 thinking when we need your very best Type 2. Follow the rules, follow the laws.

4. **Respect company property.** Your co-workers get upset if they see you wasting supplies (like paper, gloves, welding rod, toner, etc.). They don't like people making a mess, like using dirty gloves on doorways, making a mess in the breakroom, walking through the office with dirty shoes, leaving a mess in the bathroom. People spend a third of their working hours at *Org*, more than they spend awake at home. They don't want to work in a cesspool. Co-workers understand they do better if the company does better. You may be lucky enough to get to drive company equipment—forklifts, trucks, cars. Treat them as if they are your favorite aunt's. Clean it up yourself. Leave any company property

cleaner than when you found it. Remove garbage every time you exit a vehicle. Every time.

5. **Respect co-worker's property**. You would be surprised how territorial people are at work. Don't use their coffee cup (ask which one you can use), their hot sauce, or their scissors without asking. Don't sit in their chair or use their computer or PPE or water bottle. Don't use their tools.[82]

6. **Say what you are going to do and do it**. If you say you are going to do it, do it, and let your boss know when you will have it done by. If you run into a problem or an obstacle, tell someone. Ask them to help you with a solution and then finish what you said you were going to do. Every time.

7. **Take an interest – learn**. You are going to learn more than you know in your first job. No matter how long you are there, embrace it. Take it as an opportunity to get **Golden**, be your **M.E.**, and get ready for your **Maz** in the long haul. You will be working a long time, may as well learn how to do it now.

Administration

From the moment you start your job, you have to do your part to help **Org** maintain all of its processes. You cannot be the tiny piece of toe jam that brings everything to a halt. **Org** is like a computer that cannot do anything for you unless you give it all the information it needs. Like a computer, if you give **Org** a pile of garbage, you will get nothing back. Everybody in **Org** has an admin function. Think of it as a weird fairy-tale workplace with a bazillion **Goldilocks** in it.

---

82   Many hair stylists, mechanics, welders, and others use their own equipment in the workplace. It is not yours to use. They replace anything lost or stolen out of their own pockets. Expect them to be very touchy about their stuff.

Everyone needs everything just right.

People are not being buttheads about it. The payroll person who puts all the data in the computer so you can get paid needs all the information so that you can get paid. The computer likely won't let Payroll *Goldi* pay you if your Social Security information or your bank account or your address or your next of kin is not entered. Sorry, not sorry. This is a grown-up world, and these very busy people do not have time to babysit you when they have a hundred other more important things to do. They have other people relying on them. Don't worry: You do not have to be perfect, but you have to try, and you have to respect other people and respect the things they have to do to get their job done. When you screw up, make sure you own up to it and say you're sorry.

Unless you're a famous athlete, actor, or singer who signs their name a jazillion times, sign your name legibly. Slow down and take the extra second to write. You are not famous. All the *Goldis* need is to be able to read who signed the *damn piece of paper*.

Let's use Payroll *Goldilocks* as an example. Payroll *Goldi* likely reports to an accountant or to human resources or to the owner. And when Payroll *Goldi* isn't doing payroll, then there are government payroll reports that have to be submitted to the government, or there are payroll deduction reports to do, or maybe Payroll *Goldi* only does payroll part-time while spending most of the time billing customers and making sure the company gets paid so the company can keep paying the staff. Of the one trillion things Payroll *Goldi* has to do, there is no time to chase your sorry butt around trying to get your banking information so they can deposit your paycheck into the bank or figuring out which pension option or healthcare option you want to choose. You do not have the right to ruin Payroll *Goldi's* day.

All information delivered just like they want it and when they want it. Legibly.

People will think you are smarter if you print neatly. They will use Type 1 thinking.

There is more to admin than just payroll. Remember all the information zooming around *Org* we looked at in Chapter 10. Remember: on time, like they want it. Make it legible, write clearly. I

210

recommend printing in UPPERCASE LETTERS—it is not shouting if you are filling in a form for work. People generally print better when they use uppercase letters.

Admin is helping the existing processes flow through *Org* without you bringing it all to a halt. Don't be the one who brings anyone's job to a halt because you didn't do something you were supposed to do. It is that simple and it is that easy. It matters.

Data

Businesses are run on data, which is collected by everyone in the workplace and analyzed for decision making. Little pieces of data are collected and passed on through *Org* to the right spot where decisions are made regarding different areas. Here are just a few examples:

- Production: How many doohickeys should we make?

- Inventory: Do we have enough raw materials? When should we order more?

- Maintenance: Is everything running as it should?

- Marketing: How much did we sell?

- Quality Assurance: Is everything meeting specification?

- Safety: Did everyone get the safety training they need to ensure a safe workplace?

- Environment: Did everything get disposed of properly?

- Human Resources: Is everyone receiving their proper pay?

- Billing: Have we sent bills to our customers for what they have purchased?

- Accounts Receivable: Have we been paid for everything we have sold?

- Accounts Payable: Have we paid all our bills so we don't get the power shut off, get cut off by our raw-material supplier, or get cut off by our IT support contractor?

You have a part to play in making sure data (paperwork) is collected, forms are filled out neatly, and data is received by the proper person who needs that data. There is a big difference between just sending it to someone and making sure they receive it. If you want to be an *M.E.*, ask whomever you sent the information to if they received the information and if it was how and when they wanted it, and if there is anything you can do differently that would help them out more. They will think you are awesome!

You can be a difference maker, and everyone will know who you are if you are the neat and legible and reliable one. You can rocket to be the *M.E.* you want to be.

Communication

If data is collected in the forest, and the monkey eats it, does anyone know if the monkey is sick? Exactly. For communication to work, people have to know what they are communicating about. The communication needs to come full circle. You have to make sure the communication got to the person who is supposed to receive it. Then you need to make sure they understood it. And you have to make sure you understand what they think they understood, you need to make sure it was the right thing in the first place. Even simple communication can be tough. There are many meetings held making sure everyone understands what they all agree on.

There are three parts to communication. In your life and in the workplace:

1. What the speaker says.

2. What the listener hears.

3. What the message actually is.

Communication has been difficult for centuries, since the beginning of our modern workplace. It continues to this day. Here are some examples to help you avoid communication pitfalls in the workplace:

1. Repeat the question – "Hey Newbie, can you enter all these forms into the computer?"

   Wrong – "Yep."

   Right – "Sure, do you want me to build a spreadsheet, or is there already one you would like me to use? When do you need it done by?"

2. Repeat the answer – continued from above.

   Wrong – "OK, I will put it in a spreadsheet."

   Right – "OK, I will put it in the spreadsheet in the C: drive, and send you an email letting you know I have completed it. I will have it done by Thursday morning before your ten o'clock meeting."

3. Smile, eye contact – they will trust you more and see you as more reliable.

   Wrong – stare at floor

   Right – small smile, open eyes, raised eyebrows

4. WYSIATI – What You See Is All There Is (thank you, Dr. Daniel Kahneman).

   Wrong – "You didn't get the spreadsheet? Someone must have unplugged the computer system. It was probably Jingles. I saw Jingles coming out of the computer room."

   Right – "OK, I thought I sent the email with the spreadsheet to you. I will recheck my outbox. I will let you know what I find (immediately). Is there anything else I can do to fix it? OK, sorry. I am on it."

5. Nicknames for recognition – Give technical things a nickname to help you understand the technical thing and to show you understand what people are talking about.

> Wrong – "OK, I will take Unit 7534612 down to the repair shop and get a part for it."

> Right – "Got it, I will take that little blue frog thingy from the passenger seat of BlueBall[83] to the repair shop. I will check the unit number on it. Is there a form I give to the shop so they know what part to feed to Froggy to make it stop burping like an owl every time we use it? Should I leave your cell number with the shop so they can talk to someone smart if they need to?"

6. Use small words – Just. Use. Simple. Words.

> Wrong – "I will elucidate the company mission strategy to show the mootness of the impartiality of the evidentiary incidents to the new staff."

> Right – "Got it, I will tell the Newbies we have a safety meeting."

7. Follow up.

> Wrong –

> Right – "I got your email. I will ask Booper to help me, and I will get the files back to you by the end of the day. Does that work?"

8. Check in.

> Wrong –

> Right – "Hey just checking in; the computer crashed, and we lost the data for the last two days. Is it okay if we don't get it all entered until Monday? If you need it

---

83   With a shoutout to @QuickDickMcDick.

earlier, please give me a call so we can figure it out. Sorry for the hassle. Thanks."

9. Do business during business hours – you don't want your boss contacting you with business stuff and interrupting your weekend, so show the same courtesy and leave them alone.

> Wrong – Saturday at 3:00 p.m.: "We are going to lose Big Customer Inc. Our product sucks!"

> Right – Monday at 8:15 a.m.: "Good morning, hope you had a great weekend. Is there any chance you could slide some of your wisdom to me? There were a couple of things last week I didn't understand. Thanks."

10. Never send anger out in email or other forms of communication – these have a way of getting passed along. Emotions do not travel well electronically.

> Wrong – "Wow, that was a tough shift. I was pissed. What was that idiot thinking? I am not doing any more of his ^&*% even if he asks me. Are you at the wedding yet?"

> Right –

There are endless blogs on communication, and you would be well served to read a new one every month. Communication is a delicate skill, and some of the oldest and most senior people in the company may be the ones who break all the rules given above. It is **Normal**. Stick to your fundamentals. Be **Golden**, be **Mean**. You want to be reliable and trustworthy. It's a long journey.

Modes of Communication

The workplace is still settling in with the new electronic modes of communication, and it is easy to fall down into an electronic tarpit when you are trying hard not to fall into an electronic tarpit. No one wants to do that. It can be really hard to get the tar out of your hair, and it can stick under your nails forever.

Choosing the right mode of communication can be as important as the message you are trying to deliver. Do you handwrite (print) a note, phone, leave a voicemail, send an instant message, send an email, send a text, or send a group text/email? The answer is most certainly, "It depends." It depends on what the message is and who you are sending the message to. There are more exceptions to the rules than rules themselves.

Deliver emotional messages in person. Whether you are apologizing or saying thanks, it means more with your bare face hanging out.

The more complex the communication, the more personal it should be—a phone call or a face-to-face meeting is better to try to figure out a problem.

Deliver data efficiently. Be concise and use simple words. Remember *WYSIATI*, no matter what mode you are using.

Written

Again, I highly recommend printing in UPPERCASE LETTERS if you are writing something out using a pen or a pencil. It tends to look more adult than lowercase letters, unless your printing is very neat. Take your time—it is not a race. Spending some time practicing is not as goofy as it sounds. People relate neatness to intelligence.

Verbal

Even though you are speaking directly to them, remember to make eye contact and smile. Repeat either what you said or what you heard. Asking for or suggesting the next step is another way to confirm that everyone is on the same page. Just saying "Ya" is close to useless.

Phone

Some people hide behind their phones and never answer. Some let everything go to voicemail. Some people really appreciate people who will take the time to make a phone call or who will answer the phone. It is a great opportunity for you to look *Golden*. Just be polite and be honest. It you don't know something, you don't know something. If you are going to get back to someone, then get back to them.

Electronic

Email is maybe one generation old. In most workplaces, it has not been around for twenty-five years. Texts even less. Smartphones came out around twenty years ago; the iPhone reached one million users in 2007. It is easier to learn the subtleties of a Beethoven concerto than it is to learn the subtleties of finessing a group email to six different people all from different backgrounds and cultures telling them they need to change the way they are doing things. Emotions are hard to communicate in electronic communication—except anger, which comes through loud and clear. Don't be angry in electronic communications. Electronic communication is for quick, simple communication during business hours. Good luck.

Communication is a huge opportunity to set yourself apart and be *Golden*. No matter the mode of communication, here are four habits that will set you apart:

- Answer your phone. Don't make the person leave a voicemail.

- Return the text/email/voicemail. People are coming to you for help, or they are coming to you because they need something from you that is just right.

- Do what you say you are going to do.

- Contact people when you said you were going to contact them and how you were going to contact them. Even if just to say, "Hey, sorry, not quite done yet, it will be another week. My bad."

Communication is a gift, and it is very *Normal*. Not every email, text, or phone call will go as expected, or as desired. Remember, make sure the speaker and the listener agree on what the message is. "OK" isn't good enough.

If you can watch for the four parts of the job (duties, administration, data, and communication), you will be ahead of 90 percent of the other people who are starting out in their careers. Knowing what to look for, knowing what to try to accomplish, is more than half the battle. It can start on Day One, and you can build a great foundation for your *Maz*.

Day One

There are a bunch of stressful days in your life. They are all still **Normal**. Day One on the job can be one of the most stressful, anxious, good or bad, exciting days you will have. You choose. Just don't pee on the floor. It is going to happen, and it will be either good or bad, but probably mostly good. And if it is bad, it will likely get better. **Normal**.

Many people show up completely unprepared. They seem to think they have succeeded because they walked through the door. You can do so much better than them. We are going to make a plan (see Table 13.1) of how we are going to get ready to get to work on our first day, with a backup plan. We are going to dress right and we are going to act right.

It is always good to have a system—make a plan. Even if the plan goes to hell immediately, it is better than no plan at all.

"A good plan today is better than a perfect plan tomorrow."

—US General George S. Patton

Figure 13.2 has a sample for "My first day at Buy-a-Bunch," which is this Saturday from 8 a.m. to noon. I know the HR person is Bob, and I have his phone number. I will call him immediately if anything comes up (like I get a flat tire), and I have my boss's number. I am going to leave at 7:30 a.m., even though it should only be a fifteen-minute drive. I can pull into the parking lot at the park down the street if I am too early, and I can check my *social meds*. I will arrive five to ten minutes early. I have written down four questions I need to get answered. I really need to make sure I don't have any shifts for the last week of next month because of the wedding. I have checked with Uncle Hefter and he will be home so I can call him if the car takes a dump on the way, and he should still be able to get me there on time. I have made a list of what I need to take, and I have all the information for the HR department.

Table 13.1 – First Day Checklist

Name: _____   Date _____

Position: _____   HR Contact _____   Ph: _____

Employer: _____   Boss _____   Ph: _____

Getting There

Mode (circle one)	Walk	Bike	Bus	Ride	Drive

Shift Time	_____ to _____			
Date	_____		Questions	
Leave Home	_____ am pm		1 _____	
Travel Time	_____ hrs/min		2 _____	
Arrive Time	_____		3 _____	
Backup Travel Plan	_____		4 _____	
Lifeline	_____		5 _____	
Ph Number	_____			

Pay		Supplies	
Pay	_____ $/hr	Pen	_____
Hrs	_____ hrs	Resume/ Info	_____
Gross Pay	_____ $	Ph Charger	_____
Net Pay	_____	H2O Bottle	_____
		PPE	_____
		Food	_____

219

Table 13.2 – First Day Checklist Example

Name: _MC_

Date _3/23/2021_

Position: _Cashier_

HR Contact _Bob_   Ph: _123-456-7890_

Employer: _Buy a Bunch_

Boss _Betty_   Ph: _123-456-7891_

Getting There

Mode (circle one)	Walk	Bike	Bus	Ride	(Drive)

Shift Time	_____ to _____		
Date	_____	Questions	
Leave Home	_7:30_ (am) pm	1 _Breaks_	
Travel Time	_25_ hrs/min	2 _Days off For Cousins Wedding_	
Arrive Time	_7:55 am_	3 _Extra Shifts_	
Backup Travel Plan	_____	4 _Payroll Info_	
Lifeline	_Uncle Heffer_	5 _Who do I send time cards to_	
Ph Number	_123-333-4444_		

Pay		**Supplies**	
Pay	_12.00_ $/hr	Pen	_✓_
Hrs	_4_ hrs	Resume/ Info	_✓_
Gross Pay	_48.00_ $	Ph Charger	_✓_
Net Pay	_33.60_	H2O Bottle	_N/A_
		PPE	_N/A_
		Food	_✓_

Yes, that may seem a little over the top. It may seem a little juvenile, even a waste of time. But it is less stressful. Better juvenile and successful than falling on your face on the first day. You may want to adjust the page or add to it. It is definitely worth filling this out, so you don't have to think about anything on the first morning. You can just consult your sheet and go get 'er done.

Workplace Fashion

Let's talk about fashion for a quick minute. This isn't hard. What do you wear on your first job? We live in a relaxed society that appears to be accepting of wearing whatever you want to the workplace. This is not true, and if you are going to be **Golden**, you are going to take the time to figure it out. You are going to be judged—quickly, efficiently, and not necessarily accurately. It would suck if you were totally awesome but some buttbug discounts you because you start with a fashion mistake. It is straightforward and easy.

Opportunity – People judge each other quickly and efficiently in the workplace. Too many people dress like slobs. By dressing just a bit nicer—clean, no rips, reasonably fitting—you can stand way above the crowd. It doesn't have to cost a bunch of money.

- **Odor** – Before you worry about your clothes, worry about your smell. Sorry, not sorry. You need to wear deodorant. In the North American workplace, it is imperative. There is no wiggle room. Body odor is not acceptable. Everyone has a bad day or puts on the wrong shirt in the morning. That is **Normal**, and you will survive. But always having body odor is not acceptable.

- **Odor** – After you put on your clothes, worry about your smell. Sorry, not sorry. Step away from the perfume. Step away from the cologne. Work is not a cocktail party—unless you are hired to work at cocktail parties. Perfumes and colognes can be very irritating in the workplace. Your goal at work is to smell like nothing. Save the essence for the weekend.

- **Dental hygiene** – Brush your teeth. Breath can be as big an obstacle as body odor. Young adults tend to forget to go see their dentist. Go see your dentist. It is part of your *Maz*. Chew some gum or suck a breath mint before you walk through the door on Day One just in case you sipped some vile, cold Starbucks brew that smells like the cold coffee on your third-grade teacher's desk. Make sure you get rid of the gum before you go inside.

- **Fashion** – Dress for the job. Whether you are wearing jeans, slacks, a skirt, or a dress, they should be suitable for where you work. You are not dressing to go to a rave, to the beach, or to the bar. No little black dresses, yoga pants, skinny jeans, or jeans hanging halfway down your ass. Dressing wrong makes people stand a little further away from you. You shall be judged. Did we mention that?

  - You are an adult, and you are expected to wear clothes that are not wrinkled. Ironing is not difficult, and you don't have to be perfect. You just can't be completely wrinkled. New dress shirts need to be ironed so they don't look like they were just pulled out of the package.

  - Your tribe may think your T-shirts are hilarious and awesome with all your funny sayings and witty slogans. Nope. Not in the workplace, especially not on Day One. Eventually, you can wear your team colors or a jersey. Not Day One. No holes, no rips, and make sure shirts sort of fit. Tucked is still better than untucked.

  - No shoulders, no tummies, no buttcracks, no boobies. Keep them all covered, even if you are working in the warehouse, even if you have a cute belly button ring or you are really proud of your tattoo. A basketball jersey is not suitable clothing for work unless work is playing basketball. If you must wear a basketball jersey, wear a T-shirt under it.

- Whether you got a pedicure or not, wear closed-toed shoes. No flip flops. No socks and sandals. People notice other people's shoes, especially in an office setting. New and moderate is better than toe-hanging-out-of-a-hole old and expensive. DO NOT wear dirty footwear in an office. Just because the company buys you steel-toed work boots does not mean you can parade through the office getting mud and guck everywhere. If you have an office job and work in an office, you may want to put just a bit of extra money into your shoes. For some weird reason, people over-weight your shoes when they judge you. You don't need designer shoes, but they should be a little newer and well maintained. New shoelaces help.

- Pants should not have holes in them—even if that is considered stylin'. It will likely look goofy in five more years—and there will be pictures. If you work in an office setting, you can get by with average department store pants and shirts. The pants should fit reasonably well. No hanging down your arse. No riding up your arse. They should be relatively wrinkle-free.

  Ironing – It doesn't have to be perfect. It is a huge way to stand out. Grab your timer and iron for fifteen minutes while you are watching a movie or a game on a Sunday. Boom.

- Belts should be the same color as your shoes. Unless you are uber-fashiony. But if you are just trying to be *Mean* on your first day, keep it simple.

- Shirts are the first piece of clothing other people notice and judge. Non-wrinkled is the number-one priority (OK, after clean and odor free). If you are in an office setting, spending money on a tailor to fit average shirts presents you more favorably than ill-fitting expensive shirts. If you are in a casual or industrial setting where you get dirty, then be odor free. If your company provides you with uniforms, then do your part to keep them clean and odor free.

- If you need to wear a tie to the office, be **Mean**. Be average. No wild ties until you get the flow of the place. And then if you have landed in an office that likes people with a bit of flair, then you can wear your wild ties. But to start, average. If you have to wear a tie, then use a Windsor knot. Period. They look professional. Google it. Check out the videos on YouTube. Practice. It sucks. It is an opportunity to impress.

- If you are working in a dirty, sweaty environment, you get a pass on some of this. But not as much as you expect. You don't need to walk into the front office all dirty, hot, and sweaty. Gross is still gross. People want to work with people who are neat and tidy. People who seem less offensive and more trustworthy and credible. No matter what.

- If you think you need to wear a dress or a skirt, please wear one that is suitable to hang out with your grandmother's tea buddies. At least close to the knee, if you must show your knee. No slits. No low-cut blouses, please. Steer away from loud clothing or uber-fashiony clothing until you know the place. Slacks or skirts with blouses and a cardigan or jacket. No rips in the jeans, no matter how stylish that is. No four-inch heels. Flats or low heels for the first while.

- Backpacks/briefcases—clean, relatively new. If you have spent your summer backpacking in a mud bog, please do not bring the mud bog into the office. If your backpack has forty-seven collectible stuffies, please remove them for your first few days. One or two is okay. A university logo or a team logo is okay. Profanity or politics should be removed.

The great part of the whole "What do you wear to work?" thing is it is a huge opportunity. A lot of people look like slobs, and they get treated like it. People judge them quickly, efficiently, not necessarily accurately. Putting just a bit of effort into your appearance so you look credible and trustworthy is huge. Not "break the bank wear designer stuff" at work. Just clean, ironed, odor-free, and reasonably fitting tops, bottoms, and shoes. A decent belt. Average jeans or business khakis. Everyone is on a budget. You can totally stand out just by being **Mean**. And with people judging you quickly and efficiently, they may put you ahead of the five other people who have just started at the company wearing last year's skinny jeans. Take the time to be an **M.E.** and be presentable. That probably means you are more trustworthy and do better work than the Slobette Twins.

Irony – We are very casual now, but people judge you if you are casual. Quickly, efficiently, but not necessarily accurately.

PEELS – Meeting People

Now you have arrived, you chewed some gum and got rid of it, or sucked on a breath mint. You have walked in and get sent to HR. You are waiting for Bob or Betty to show up. You are sitting in the general office, and the receptionist is there. Remember, just like you judged him or her, he or she is judging you. Are you safe and trustworthy? Are you going to help out around here, or are you going to be gone after the first shift or by the end of the first week? You don't have to hit a home run or belt out a hit single to get on the right side of **Normal** with the receptionist. Just be **Mean**. Be **Golden**. Be average. Here are the five things to remember:

- **P – Pen**: Have a pen and your personal info/resume. You may have more forms to fill out. Don't make them scurry around for you. Yes, there may be a million pens. Or there may not be. Have your own and show them you have thought about it. You respect their time and you are not helpless.

- **E – Engage**: Be ready to talk to the staff if they do not seem overly busy. "How is your day?" "Nice office, how long have you

225

been working here?" Look them in the eyes, maybe raise your eyebrows a bit, or make sure you open your eyes—it makes you seem interested. Stay positive—"Ya, traffic wasn't bad." "Always interesting people on the bus."

- **E – Empathy**: Remember, that person is likely just as nervous about meeting you as you are about meeting them. Remember that with each person you meet that day. Cut them some slack, smile, be thankful. Consider they have already given you something. They have given you an opportunity and they want your help.

The zygomaticus muscle is the muscle that pulls up the sides of your mouth when you smile. Use it.

- **L – Listen**: Maintain eye contact and keep your eyes open. Maybe a slight smile and use your zygomaticus muscle. You also may get some interesting information. ("Betty can be pretty harsh at first, but once you get over that she is awesome to work for.")

- **S – Smile**: It cannot be said enough. Smile. Not a wide, grinning, idiot smile. But a small, wise, knowing smile that shows you are an adult, in an adult situation, and you are going to be fine. It will all be *Normal*.

PEELS is the order of the day for Day One, and it is not a bad idea for the rest of your days as well.

Summary

You already knew everything in this chapter. We just gave it some struc-ture. There were many details, but they all came down to the same set of fundamentals you already have in place. Be **Mean**, be **Golden**. Make your Mom proud.

You understand the job matters because it is the job that is going to help you meet your goal of staying away from harm, hunger, and homeless-ness. You are going to put some effort into the job, and you are going to engage with the other staff because you know they want your help, and if you help them, they are going to respect you. You know that you are going to be **Golden** in the workplace. You are not going to be a deficient dipshit, nor are you going to overdo it in the workplace and flame out like five-dollar fireworks. Your career is a journey, and it will last most of your life. It will define who you are, starting with the first, part-time, bottom-of-the-ladder, minimum-wage job.

You know how to attend to the four parts of the job—the duties, the administration, the data, and the communication. You understand that everyone has a bit of **Goldilocks** in them because they all have jobs to do, and they need everything just right so they can do their part and not chase you around for not doing your part. They aren't being poopybums. They just care.

You are going to make a plan for Day One, and you are going to dress appropriately. You are not going to stink or smell. You are going to get your **Mean** on and dress kinda average. Definitely clean, trustworthy, and credible. And when you walk through that door, you are going to **PEELS** back your layers and accept it. You are an adult. Welcome. We appreciate you showing up. We need your help.

CHAPTER 14
Getting That Job

If you have finished the rest of the chapters, then you are all set to get a job. Getting a job is just a simple process ending with starting on Day One. This is simple and mechanical. Just go through the process. Use your timer where necessary. Understand the person hiring is the ultimate *Goldilocks*. They need what they need when they need it and exactly how they need it. There are lots of opportunities for you if you can do that. If you move fast and legibly and are trustworthy and credible, you are likely a good candidate for a job that can start you on your journey. Many, many jobs are only getting one qualified application these days. There are a bazillion job openings. This job will not be your last job. It is your first job. It is time to build on the foundation you have built.

What Do You Want to Do?

Your passion may be folding and flying paper airplanes or making goat soufflé. I don't really care. Consider that your passion won't make you enough *Pennies* for your *Pyramid* right now. Poor Poopy, or Poopsy, as the case may be. This is the first part of your career. We are building a foundation so you can move further away from harm, hunger, and homelessness. Your passion can come later once you have the first couple of levels of your *Pyramid* taken care of.

Table 14.1 has a list of 22 different areas you can work in. Have a look at what catches your eye. Put a checkmark beside the ones you like. You should be aware that within each of those broad areas, there are tons of different rewarding jobs.

Remember, we are not looking for your dream job. You should get a job before you should worry about singing *kumbaya* on top of your **Pyramid**. Yes, you may want to work in a salon or an auto body shop. Cool. Get some job experience and some skills. Be **Golden**, and then you can parlay your performance into your passion, or you can make money and pursue your passion as your pastime. Your passion may not pay you enough to have the **Maz** you want to have.

Table 14.1 – List of Potential Job Areas

Management
Business and Financial
Computer and Mathmatical
Architecture and Engineering
Life, Physical & Social Sciences
Community and Social Services Potential
Legal
Educational Instruction and Library
Arts, Design Entertainment, Sports and Media
Healthcare Practitioners and Technical
Healthcare Support
Protective Services
Food Preparation
Buildings and Grounds Cleaning and Maintenance
Personal Care and Service
Sales
Office and Administrative Support
Farming, Fishing and Forestry
Construcation and Extraction
Installation, Maintenance and Repair
Production
Transportation and Materials Moving

Buckle Down, Buckle Up, and Start the Search

Grab your timer and get your computer. Go to a jobsite (Indeed, ZipRecruiter, etc.) and enter a few of your options. Start filling out Table 14.2. Consider the jobs you think you can get, the jobs you are willing to do, and the jobs that do not seem horrible. Anything above that is a bonus. Search out companies where you think you might be able to get a job and see if there are any jobs on their website.

Cool your coolness and up your ***Mean***ness. Fill out the table below as you go through your journey. As each opportunity comes up, add it to the list. Check each box as it comes up. If it doesn't, oh well. Put a line through it.

Table 14.2 – Job Application Log

Jobs That Might Not Suck									
Date	Job Title	Company	Distance	Search	Apply	Interview	Offer	Accepted	Start Date
5/12	Clerk	Target	3 miles	✓					
5/12	Landscaper	?		✓	✓				
5/12	Fryswiththat	McD's	0.5 miles	✓	✓				
	Mechanic	?	?	✓					

Try, try, and try again, little Muffincup. There is no magic to this. You already know everything you need to know. Grab your timer and keep going. Try again.

When looking for entry-level staff, whether college graduates or not, I found myself valuing job experience from McDonald's, Target, Walmart, and Home Depot. (No, they haven't paid me for saying that.) Those jobs told me the applicant had been given some work training and could work with the public. This was compared to Auntie Mae's Cupcake Shop or Bob's Garage, which didn't really tell me anything.

If the websites aren't doing it, start asking around the old-fashioned way. Ask your parents, siblings, friends, aunts, uncles, grandparents, teachers, and coaches.

If you are really determined, and want to show your *Golden* side, make a resume and make a list of all the places you want to apply. Walk in and ask to speak the manager. Be polite.

Go back and review what you are supposed to do. Trustworthy and credible. Your odds of landing a job by *cold calling*[84] are probably better than they have ever been. There are so many jobs sitting open, and one-third to one-half of people don't show up for interviews or won't answer their phone when you try to contact them for an interview. Show your grit, your determination. Show your *M.E.*-ness.

Now that you have found some jobs that kind of strike your wee little fancy, then let's look at Table 14.3, the next form we need to fill out. This form is intended to keep track of all the personal information you are going to have to put into an application, and then likely enter into the payroll forms when you start work. You may as well compile it all together now.

---

84 Cold calling means you just call on companies unannounced. It scares the crap out of people. People respect people who can do it. It means walking through the door of a company and saying, "Hi, my name is ___, and I am wondering if there might be any job openings. Is there anyone I can talk to about that?"

Table 14.3 – Pre-Employment Checklist

Things to Do			
Thinking about applying for work	Yes	Maybe	No
Decide to apply for work	Yes	Maybe	No
Commit to apply for work	Yes	Maybe	No
Signature: _____ Date: _____			
Adult enough to get a job	Yes	Maybe	No
Gather Necessary Information & Documents			
Birth certificate	Yes	No	
Passport	Yes	No	N/A
Social Security card	Yes	No	
Work visa/green card (if needed)	Yes	No	N/A
Driver's license	Yes	No	
Driver's record	Yes	No	
Resume	Yes	No	
Ability to Pass Background Checks			
Drug (urine analysis)	Yes	No	
Drug (saliva)	Yes	No	
Drug (hair)	Yes	No	
Crime (misdemeanor)	Yes	No	
Crime (felony)	Yes	No	
DUI	Yes	No	

How Far Away Can I Work					
Miles to work	1	3	5	7	10+

Available transportation:		
Walk	Yes	No
Bike/skate/scooter	Yes	No
Public transportation	Yes	No
Car	Yes	No

Hours	Full-Time	Part-Time
Work times		
Morning	Yes	No
Afternoon	Yes	No
Evening	Yes	No
Graveyard (10PM to 8AM)	Yes	No
Weekdays	Yes	No
Weekends	Yes	No
Shift work	Yes	No

Pay Expectations			
	Wage	Salary	
Minimum wage	_____ $/hr		
Wage range	_____ $/hr -	_____ $/hr	
Union	Yes	No	
Non-union	Yes	No	
Salary range	_____ $/month	_____ $/month	

Consider the checklist as your start of being **Work-Golden**. Make it neat. Commit to it, cool your coolness, and fill it out.

Are you ready to work? Circle as appropriate. Sign your name. Legibly—unless you are really amazing, then give it that over-the-top scrawl that no one can read. (Or be **Mean** and make your signature an average, neat representation of your name, to start.)

There is a bunch of information and some documents that you may or may not need. This should be most of them. You will probably have to fill out an I-9 form when you are hired to prove you are legally able to work in the United States. Your employer will give it to you with a thousand other forms. You just fill it out and return it to them, usually on your first day, so you want to have the information handy.

You may or may not need a resume, depending on whether you are looking at a simple job, or you are a young professional just getting out of college looking for your first big job. If you need to make a resume, grab your timer, set it to ten minutes,

A resume today is better than a perfect resume tomorrow.

download a simple resume template, and fill it in. Don't overthink it. If you find it hard to do, when the timer goes off, go do something else for twenty minutes, and come back and set your timer for ten minutes. You will be half-done. Just finish the damn thing.

If you were born in the US and have lived here your entire life, you likely just need your Social Security number. Passports and other fun stuff are for those born elsewhere. The company may want to take a photocopy of your driver's license. This is most common when you are going to possibly be driving company equipment and they want to get a copy of your driver's record. The company is liable for any accidents you get in while on company business, whether in your vehicle or theirs. **Org** has deeper pockets than you, so lawyers love to include companies in lawsuits so they can get a piece of a larger **Pie**. **Org** wants to make sure you are a reasonably responsible driver. **Org** may not want to hire you if you have had a DUI. Think about that. I will wait.

Beware. More and more employers will require you to take a drug test before you start employment (Chapter 12, Wealth Killers). If that upsets you, I have placed a soap box outside of town in a field for you to go stand on and make a speech. I won't be there. I don't care. It would be sad if you came all the way through this book and got to this point only to figure out that you can't get half of the jobs because you can't pass a drug test. Sorry, not sorry. Makes it easier for everyone else. It doesn't matter what is legal and what isn't. *Org* is concerned about what is safe and what isn't. Drunk, stoned, or high people are not safe and can't keep *Org* safe or competitive. Go work somewhere else. This is especially true for the good jobs that pay better. If you can't pass a drug test, you just demoted yourself to the lowest levels of employment, if you can get hired. Way to go, Farty!

If the DUI and the drug test are not an issue, good for you. Being *Mean* has been a great investment. You are ahead of a lot of other people. Makes it easier to climb your *Maz*, and to stay there. Your *Pie* will be bigger, and you get a bigger slice.

And finally, just for some little housekeeping issues, please give it some thought of how far you can travel for work, how you will get there, and when you are available to work. It is very tiring going through a lot of effort to hire someone only to learn they can't work full time, or they can't work weekends when the job posting says "Weekends."

You can also do some of the simple math we chatted about back in Chapter 3. How much do you expect to make? Give it some thought. Have an answer. You may be starting at minimum wage, but if you are *Golden*, you won't be there long. Remember, raises are smaller than you think, and they are more valuable than you know. Good luck.

It is now time to just buckle down and get it done. It is better to get this done today than wait until you are perfect tomorrow.

If you get an interview, go back and read about your Day One in Chapter 13. All the same things apply. You got it.

If you get an offer, say, "Thank you." If you don't want the job, just be honest. Don't stiff them and say you will be there, and then not show, or go ghost on them. That is trashy.

You are the adult, and this is all in your hands now. You know everything you need to know, and hopefully you know there is lots you can learn. It will be **Normal**; it will be **Golden**; it will be awesome. So many people will appreciate you. So many people will be proud of you. Go be the **M.E.** you know you can be.

Be safe. Be smart. Take care.

You have done a helluva job getting this far. You were smart when you started this book. Now you are smart and prepared. Enjoy.

CHAPTER 15
Summary

Many years ago, you started school with your little cute face, some cute clothes, and a cool lunchbox. What has changed? You are older, smarter, and taller. You are still cute. Now you are set to enter the work world. You are not sure how that is going to go, and you are not sure what is going to happen. If you have gone through this book, you now have a plan you can use at work whether you are graduating college with a four-year degree or you are heading into the workforce straight from high school. Either way, you can have a *Normally* successful life.

By the time you went through the whole book, you ended up with a simple process to go through to get a job. You understand it may be your first few jobs, and you will have lots of time to find your career and find the right fit for you. While you are in the early part of that journey, you know the job is an intersection between you and your employer—*Org*. You are going to be several steps ahead of other people in the workplace, knowing the different components of your job: the duties, the administration, the data, and the communication. By understanding each of these functions, you will become a valued team member, and you will be invited into the work family. It will also help that you understand there is more to *Org* than a simple Org chart. You understand that *Org* is full of all these *Goldilocks*-type people who all need everything they need just right, just when they need it, and just how they need it. You understand how to flow with it all.

There are some grown-up subjects that have to be dealt with, and you now know the five wealth killers that can screw up your career and your life. You are probably still surprised at how many companies require drug testing as a pre-employment requirement, and then they perform ongoing random drug testing to provide a safe workplace for all the staff and the general public. You also now have a plan for dealing with the **SAAGS** that will happen at work. Sadness, anger, anxiety, guilt, and shame/embarrassment will happen. You know how to deal with them when they pop their ugly head into your life. It might not be pretty, and it might not be rosy, but it will keep your head above water—*Normally*.

Your ability to understand how people think and how they will judge you as soon as they see you—quickly, efficiently, but not necessarily accurately—protects you by arming you with knowledge that many others do not have and do not understand. You can see how many decisions get made using lazy Type 1 thinking when the situation really needs us to use our more analytical Type 2 thinking to make the best decision possible. Even when people use the best brain they've got, they still make mistakes by over-weighting rare events, or having biases they don't know they have, or not understanding they rely too much on things they remember easily—like all the times they did the dishes. Understanding these mistakes in the workplace can help you perform, and be *Golden*, and be the *M.E.* you want to be. You want to be the person that always gets things done the right way, not one of the people who gets things done always using Type 1 thinking—quickly, efficiently, but not necessarily accurately.

It will all be *Normal* as you go into the workplace. As simple as understanding that good things happen and bad things happen. Really good things and really bad things don't happen as often as totally average things happen. You have a lot of control over your average, and you probably realize that you want to make your average as good as you can. You can shift your average on most things. *Normally* it will be a great career and a great life.

It also helps that you have learned how to divvy up people and time and money in your head. As you cut up the *Pie*, you realize all the different options and all the different factors in any given situation. You realize that everyone and everything isn't black and white. By looking for the main factors in people, you will avoid some of the mistakes the *Kahn* talked about. You will understand that everyone overvalues their contributions, not because they are horrible people, but because it is easiest for them to remember what they did and how they contributed. It is much harder to recall how others may have helped. You can use that when you are measuring other people. You can also see how you can move your average by shifting the time you spend doing some things, and they may not be huge shifts. Ten minutes here, a half an hour there, can move your average to a better *Normal*. You can also improve your world by understanding where your money goes.

Your money is a huge part of your *Maz*, and understanding your money allows you to take care of the necessary parts of your life, like food, shelter, and safety. This helps you understand that not all your money gets spent on making you feel good about yourself. No matter how much money you make, there is a limited amount to spend on your self-esteem, and it is best if a good piece of your self-esteem *Pie* comes from working. Earning that part of your *Maz* actually pays you money to contribute, and then you can spend on the other parts of you to build a better, more solid *Pyramid*.

Your life *Pyramid* is your responsibility now that you are an adult. You will want to build your own *Pyramid,* and your career will give you the tools and the supplies to do that. Not many adults would want to leave their *Pyramid* to be built by someone else or the government, so it is best you start building yours now. This is how you will avoid harm, hunger, and homelessness.

All of this is very *on-the-rock* thinking that goes back to *Ari*. You did not need to review a bunch of university studies or do a bunch of intricate calculus to determine the path that would be best for you. *Ari* figured out that you could start out average (*Mean*), and then you could become *Golden* by learning from others and finding some *Moral Exemplars*. There is a great path for you by becoming an *M.E.* for yourself and for your family and your friends.

Please remember that you have talent, and we need your help.

Thanks in advance for showing up, for your hard work, and for your dedication. We all appreciate it.

INDEX

AUTHOR

Gary Houston is the Founder of the Center for Workforce Entry. He has used his engineering degree and his MBA to hire and mentor young people for over thirty years. He lives in Davis, CA with his wife Sallie, their two youngest children and Dogface.

ILLUSTRATOR

David Anderson worked on the editorial pages of several newspapers in South Africa as a political cartoonist before moving to Toronto with his family in 1990 where he continues to freelance. His work has appeared in most of Canada's major daily papers and has been syndicated internationally. He has written and illustrated children's books, does corporate caricatures and graphics, along with advertising and storyboards. Two of his books, *Whispers from the African Bush* and *More Tales from the African Bush* are currently available on Amazon.

When not involved with his art, he can often be found photographing birds and other local wildlife.

CPSIA information can be obtained
at www.ICGtesting.com
Printed in the USA
LVHW031801140223
739491LV00002B/324